CREATE A MENTOR CULTURE

HOW TO MENTOR WITH HEART AND START A RIPPLE EFFECT

HELEN PATTERSON

CONTENTS

GRATITUDE AND APPRECIATION

Back in 2017 at the end of my last corporate role, I felt compelled to research and write about my experiences and passion for mentoring. This book is the result.

While this is a "business" book, I'd like to think about it as the start of an undeniable urge to do something more with this life. And so here we are at the end of a years-long journey that is no doubt only the beginning of more writing and self-discovery.

Lately, the Acknowledgement section has moved to the back perhaps because many people skip over this part. For me, however, this is one of the best parts of a book. It is an attempt to show gratitude and appreciation to a multitude of people who help shape not only the content of the words on the page but the person creating them. It is also a small satisfying ode to the humans who made it happen.

So here I go.

First, I thank my parents, Karolina and Zdzislaw (Stan) whose humble beginnings I now appreciate even more deeply. Thanks for my life, and for co-creating me. I'm hoping you are proud as you look down from heaven upon your future generations.

Next, my incredible family. Thanks to my husband Tim, and children, Katie and Cullen—I know I can be a lot sometimes! You inspire me daily and I appreciate all of your support and love. Always. To the moon and back! And to Joey, our tiny goldendoodle, my shadow, who taught me what unconditional love and pure joy is. Can't wait to see what's next in all of our lives together.

To my siblings, Donna, Steven and Krysia, and Richard who we have since lost, thanks for putting up with me all these years, and for teaching me that happiness can be found in many surprising ways. We all turned out okay didn't we? And yes I will keep going (haha). And to my extended family on both sides, I feel so blessed to know you're also in my corner and cheering me on!

To the many people I interviewed for the book, over 50 wonderful humans! While I could not include everyone, know that your input and inspiration is embedded within and I am thankful for your willingness to share some of your mentorship experiences with me. Huge hugs to all of you.

To my editor and book coach, Helen Wilkie, aka the "other Helen". We had so many stops and starts, our life events and interruptions as we navigated this process together. You guided me from ideas, outlines and first words on the page to final manuscript. As I've said, two Helens are better than one! And I could not have done it without you. Thanks for your patience, the countless reviews and for hanging in with me to the end.

To Laura Beauparlant and Maria Sanchez of Lab Creative who designed the beautiful cover and all the Life Works Well branding, thank you for capturing the essence of mentoring with heart and the ripple effect of mentorship. So grateful to work with both of you. And thanks to Stephen Velasco, Jasmine Barta and Emeline Lambert who helped with the behind-the-scenes book launch marketing strategy, website content and social media.

To the early readers and my team at Life Works Well, I could not have done any of this without you. And especially to Juanita Christmas, Joanne Kane and Emeline Lambert, who provided valuable suggestions, incredible input and emotional support along the way! And to Karen Dean, my accountability partner, thank you for the pep talks and sharing the writing journey with me.

And to my dear friend and colleague Elizabeth Williams who reviewed early versions and was one of my greatest fans. You didn't get to see the final version before you passed—I finally did it and got the "damn thing done". Thank you for encouraging me to finish. Miss you.

To the many mentees and mentors I've been fortunate to have in my life—especially Sania Sanzgiri, Lavanya Mathur, Nora Spinks and Philip Wilson, and to the coaches who have been there for me when this was only an idea—Jenna Smith, Jill Valentine, Ariana McNally and Eleanor Beaton.

To my local book club gals and friends, you make reading together so much fun, and I learn so much from each of you (Christine, Janice, Jen E, Jenn M, Karney, Sue, Tanya and Tara). And finally, to my girlfriends from high school (Andrea, Kim, Janice, Michelle and Patty) and law school (Candace, Damhnait, Judy, Julie, Laura, Leanne, Lisa and Lynne), you have inspired me to make a contribution to the world I'm very proud of. We've all grown, laughed and cried together. You are my everyday mentors and part of starting the ripple effect to create a mentor culture and world. Let's keep it going!

FOREWORD

Success is often misunderstood. You can't do it alone.

Many believe it is achieved by acquiring more degrees, landing a dream job, working long hours, or trying to outdo others. However, true success is not about these external markers. Instead, success in life and work is deeply rooted in relationships. To be successful, everyone needs people who believe in them, invest in them, and encourage them.

Mentors, coaches, sponsors, colleagues, bosses and peers, competitors, clients/customers, family and friends all impact your path to success, happiness and wellbeing. To achieve success, attain career advancement, reach your full potential and flourish at home and work, you need to continuously learn and grow from your experiences, know yourself well, leverage your strengths, engage in lifelong learning and self-discovery, and make conscious decisions about your family and career, and the interface between your work and life.

Personal and professional relationships are critical for building your capacity, competence, and confidence.

You build **capacity** from experience, learning from those experiences and observing others, reflecting on mistakes and celebrating accomplishments (yours and other people's) balancing multiple responsibilities and commitments, navigating complex organizational systems, managing workplace politics, and capitalizing on the organizational culture.

You build **competence** by acquiring technical skills through observation, listening and learning, whether in a class, on a course, on the job, or at a conference.

You build **confidence** from within, often with the help of others who see more in you than you see in yourself. Confidence allows you to take on stretch assignments, ask questions, seek advice, try new things, take calculated risks, withstand criticism and rejection, and accept compliments.

In this book, author Helen Patterson untangles the confusion around mentorship, coaching, and sponsorship. She provides a clear and comprehensive guide to understanding these concepts and how these relationships can be effectively utilized to foster personal and professional growth.

Whether you are designing or redesigning your mentorship initiatives, want more from your relationships, or are a mentor, mentee, coach, coaching client, sponsor, or sponsee, you will find valuable insights in the following informative chapters.

Over the years, I have worked with Helen in several capacities, including as a vendor, colleague, and mentor, when she applied her skills as a lawyer, leader and mentor in corporate and non-profit environments. She is a competent, hard-working professional with a growth mindset and a deep commitment to wellbeing. Helen's conversational style is personable, her ideas are inspirational, her writing is clear, and her stories are engaging. She does extensive research and draws from a wealth of experience and knowledge to provide practical advice and real-world examples that illustrate the power of mentorship and its impact on your life and career.

As you read this book, you will discover that success is not a solitary journey. It is a collaborative effort that involves building and nurturing relationships. You will learn how to work with mentors and be in traditional, reverse and reciprocal mentor relationships. This book will show you how to build supportive relationships to achieve your goals and flourish in life and work.

Create a Mentor Culture demystifies mentorship with actionable strategies that will transform countless careers and lives.

Nora Spinks,

CEO of Work-Life Harmony Enterprises

A highly sought-after mentor to executives and professionals in every sector and diverse workplaces across Canada and around the world.

INTRODUCTION

Throughout my younger life I felt like I was always walking on eggshells. Quietly tiptoeing around my home and environment in one of the Toronto projects so as not to get into trouble. For years, I struggled to fit in, to feel like I belonged. I went from a straight A student in grade school and my first couple of years of high school to almost flunking out in Grade 11. I was lost, getting involved in extracurricular activities that were not good for me.

A wake-up call, a scary trip to the guidance office, set me back on track. This was a pattern I lived for many years with the limited guidance I received (or allowed myself to receive).

My personal and career path was not the easiest, straight-line journey. I came from a low-income family, my parents new immigrants to Canada, who were both what I call "children of the war". They didn't have the best experiences growing up, and some of that was passed on to me and my four siblings. For some reason, though, I managed to break a bit of the cycle by putting myself through university, the first in my family to do so. It was tough. It was a ton of work. Often, I didn't have anyone I could turn to or ask for advice. The occasional inspirational teachers, some good friends, and some wonderful mentors later in life helped me become the person I am today.

As a result of these experiences, when I did receive mentorship it changed my life. It helped me establish my belief that everyone should have a mentor throughout each stage of life and throughout their careers. A world with mentors for all is a better world, where everyone is lifted up to their full potential. Imagine the possibilities if every child, every teen, every student, every adult and every employee had the opportunity to learn and grow from someone else. That is the world I envision.

My earliest mentoring experiences were with organic mentors where the relationship started naturally and eventually ended up becoming either a formal traditional or reciprocal mentorship. One of the best mentors I ever had was Nora Spinks, who I referred to as the "work-life guru" of Canada. She was someone who inspired me and guided me as I started my first foray into entrepreneurship. Nora ran a company called Work Life Harmony and I worked with her as a client when I was a senior leader in HR at a large financial institution, and I was fortunate to be mentored and learn from her. I worked on several projects with Nora as I shadowed her and helped with her business and clients. To this day she is one of my role models and friends. I'm honoured to have her in my extended family.

Fast forward to almost 10 years later, when I met a young woman at my last traditional corporate job. She was a kindred spirit and old soul, and what started as a special friendship at work turned into reciprocal mentoring where each of us learned from each other. You'll hear more about Lauren Charbon in the chapter discussing organic and reciprocal mentoring. We continue to meet to support each other in our journeys in life and career. You can find mentors everywhere.

My vision is a world where parents are the first positive mentors to their children, and teachers are the next best mentors to their students, a world where in the workplace all employees work with a mentor, not simply the high potentials (HIPOs) or the emerging leaders or the chosen few. Mentoring has been in place for centuries, starting with the first mentor of Telemachus, whose name of course was Mentor. Yet, it seems the world and the people in this world have not discovered the benefits that come from a meaningful and authentic mentor relationship.

Unfortunately, this vision isn't the reality today.

Why is it that only a few special teachers in elementary and secondary schools make a strong impact on youth? These teachers are holding the future leaders of the world in their hands, and have an opportunity to help make a huge difference in the lives of these young learners. Yet, statistics don't bear out success in the world of Academia. In parts of our planet, young children don't even have the opportunity to have an education, particularly young girls. Imagine what the world would look like if every child had the right to an excellent education, with wonderful mentor teachers inspiring them to learn and to grow and to give to others. At the time of publishing this book, Mentor Canada, which is doing amazing work, states that 15,000 young people are looking for mentors.[1]

Higher education may be doing slightly better but I think the jury is out on that one. Graduates from College and University in Canada, and abroad, are struggling to find meaningful work and perhaps it's because there has been a failure to provide mentorship opportunities here to these young adults to help them succeed.[2]

There are 46 million young people, aged 8-18, living in America and 16 million of them are growing up without a mentor. That's one out of every three young people who, outside of their family at home, don't have a trusted adult they believe they can turn to for advice and guidance. Of those young people, nine million face a variety of day-to-day challenges that put them at risk for falling off track.[3]

Mentoring creates meaningful connections that can positively impact the lives of both mentor and mentee. Those who receive mentorship are more likely to see improved academic, social, and economic prospects. Those who mentor are able to further build important leadership, management and creative skills, while giving back to their community.

That means that *EVERY* mentorship matters.

In Canada:

Young adults who had access to mentoring (any mentor) while they were growing up were more likely to report the following positive outcomes than non-mentored youth. They were:

- *53% more likely to report good or excellent mental health;*
- *Over two times more likely to report a very or somewhat strong sense of belonging;*
- *Over twice as likely to have completed high school;*
- *95% more likely to have pursued further education after high school;*
- *59% more likely to have an occupation (either employed and/or studying);*
- *More likely to report feeling positive about their career planning;*
- *More likely to report having strong social capital.*[4]

The workplace isn't any better unless you're a Fortune 500 company where 84% of them have mentor programs.[5] In the entrepreneurial world, the majority of the leaders have indicated that they owe much of their success to a mentor. So why then isn't this widespread? Why are the success stories that the everyday person hears about coming from the 1% who already hold most of the globe's wealth? Why can't more people learn from their success too? If the return on investment from paid coaching or business mentors and corporate programs pay huge dividends, why aren't more individuals and companies engaging in mentorship frequently?

I believe it comes down to a typical problem, a failure to execute well. Throughout this book I share some of my research on how organizations can yield positive returns by implementing mentor programs and how to do it right. For example, one study demonstrated over 80% of retention of employees for both mentors and mentees who participated in a pilot mentoring program that was later rolled out to the entire organization.

Today, I mentor young entrepreneurs, often women, on a volunteer basis. I also mentor many HR and new professionals who lack the confidence to step into their leadership and influence decision-makers within their organization. I also help companies implement successful mentoring programs as most tend not to create the benefits that could exist. Through my research, my interviews and my experiences I've come to learn what works and what doesn't when it comes to effective, productive and joyful mentoring that creates meaningful experiences and lasting relationships. It is all about mentoring with heart.

Hopefully this book will help you design a mentor culture. I hope it also helps individuals who might like to find a mentor or coach. Or perhaps it will inspire you to mentor someone else and share your knowledge. If we all gave in this way, I'm truly convinced it would change your life, those within your organization and people across our beautiful earth.

Ideally, organizations can also benefit from this knowledge across the globe and create some understanding and truth in the hundreds of mentor quotes I read. Everyone deserves a mentor and should eventually become one. We learn from each other. We grow together. This truth in simple terms is that everyone's success is impacted by some form of mentorship.

If you are fortunate enough to have an excellent mentor experience, then it will be evident. The majority of Fortune 50 to 500 companies have a mentor program. There are several business cases that prove better career or life success with a mentor or coach. If the experience has not been meaningful or very disillusioning, I'll give some tips to help you address that too. Let's make a small difference in someone's life by being an individual mentor. Better yet, let's make a huge difference in many people's lives by bringing these mentor programs into all workplaces and communities so generations after us will thrive!

Being an everyday mentor is all about finding a connection with another person and then working to create a relationship where both give and grow together.

There is something for everyone in this book. For history buffs, you will find a history of mentoring and how it has evolved over the years. As I researched for this book, I had a lot of questions about how a mentor compares to other types of relationships such as coaches or sponsors or managers and I try to help differentiate them. Many say mentoring is on the decline, and yet numbers of leaders indicate they owe some of their success to having a mentor. The roles of coach and sponsor have definitely grown in the last decade. In my view all of these programs or relationships provide huge value to the career or personal growth of any individual.

You can also learn about the categories of mentoring, from traditional, to peer, to reciprocal and reverse, there is a myriad of mentor relationships. You need to find the right one for you and the right type of program for your organization. It is important to understand the roles of a mentor, as they may change depending on the situation. Equally important is the role of a mentee and you'll discover some guidance to include in your program education. For business leaders who know the value of mentoring but haven't figured out how to create programs that benefit everyone in the organization, this book will set you up for future success as I discuss how to create a mentor culture, the business case and provide some valuable resources.

I hope that you find something here that will motivate you to become a mentor in the future, or seek out a mentor if you don't have one. And if you are able to implement mentor programs in your workplace, and then also give back to your community then you'll have helped make the world a better place! If we connect with each other, learn from each other, and share our unique knowledge and talents one person or one group at a time, we will all grow and create a better workplace and an even better world. Are you ready to create a mentor culture, mentor with heart and become an everyday mentor? It's never too late to start. And the ripple effect will be felt.

1

WHAT IS MENTORSHIP AND HOW DOES IT DIFFER FROM OTHER SUPPORTIVE RELATIONSHIPS?

"A mentor is someone who allows you to see the hope inside yourself. A mentor is someone who allows you to know that no matter how dark the night, in the morning joy will come.

"A mentor is someone who allows you to see the higher part of yourself when sometimes it becomes hidden to your own view."

—*Oprah Winfrey*

Mentorship has a rich history, stretching back for centuries. The word "stretching" makes sense, as it describes what can happen to each of the participants in a mentor relationship: both participants will stretch their knowledge, their relationship and their being.

They will expand and grow—heart, mind, body and soul.

The traditional definition of a mentoring relationship is one in which a more experienced (typically more 'senior') person provides advice and guidance to a younger person. Picture the wise old owl with the youngling, sharing insights and helping the *owlet* develop new skills and experience. As a Harry Potter fan, I liken this to the relationship between Dumbledore and Harry, although this can also be depicted as a reciprocal mentorship, as Harry taught Dumbledore a few things too.

The Oxford Dictionary defines a mentor as "an experienced and trusted advisor." Two of the key ingredients to a successful mentor relationship are trust and connection. In a company, the experienced person educates and counsels employees, while the person with expertise in an academic setting does the same for students. And there are mentors that may come along at any stage of our life and career journey.

Leaders such as Simon Sinek, Oprah Winfrey and Bill Gates credit their mentors with some of their success. Now, there is a movement towards other supportive relationships, such as coaching and sponsorship, and we'll touch on these as well. I believe the mentorship relationship is special and extremely beneficial to one's success.

The word "mentor" was inspired by the character of the same name in Homer's classic novel *The Odyssey*, which chronicles the journey of Odysseus back home in the years following the Trojan War. While he is making his way back, the goddess Athena appears to his son, Telemachus, in the form of an old family friend, Mentor, to offer him support and guidance in his father's absence. Their interactions in *The Odyssey* represent one of the earliest examples of mentorship.

In *The Odyssey*, Mentor meets the traditional definitions of a mentor:

- a loyal adviser of Odysseus entrusted with the care and education of Telemachus
- a wise and trusted counsellor or teacher
- an influential senior sponsor or supporter.

I love an interview between B. R. J. O'Donnell and Professor Gregory Nagy, a classics professor at Harvard University, describing how the bond between Telemachus and his mentor remains relevant today. Professor Nagy discusses what the story of the original Mentor reveals about our understanding of personal and professional guidance even thousands of years later.[1]

According to Professor Nagy, in the Greek language of *The Odyssey*, a mentor is someone who instills a heroic mentality in somebody.

I love that idea. We all need someone to help lift us up and believe in our abilities, and that's exactly what Athena (in the form of Mentor), as the goddess of intelligence, does in her relationship with Telemachus. She arrives at a time when Telemachus's life is very misdirected and he's not sure about anything.

There is a part in the book where at the council of the gods, Athena lays out her intent to put "menos" into Telemachus. Nagy explains that this Greek word is usually translated as "heroic strength," but "menos" is not just strength of any kind—it is mental strength. "By that I mean the kind of surge of power you feel in being able to put things into action. Hence the connection between "menos" and mentor: a mentor is someone who gives mental strength to someone else. In the world of *The Odyssey*, without good intentions there cannot be mentorship."[2]

We all need our own Athena—and I mean everyone, not only the chosen few. While we will have people in our lives who inspire us in many ways through different relationships, for me the mentor relationship is the most impactful.

The Big Three

Many people use the words "mentor", "sponsor" and "coach" interchangeably, and this has led to confusion. I outline below some level-setting explanations of how a mentor differs from a coach, as well as from a sponsor. This clarity will then help you decide what type of program is important in your organization, and when to work with each. The timing is important, as are resources.

Some organizations might have programs for all three types of relationship, all at once or at different times. I will share an excellent methodology for program implementation later on. We will also review some other important relationships that serve unique and important purposes for professional and personal growth.

Let's take a look at the three main forms of relationship in the workplace: mentorship, coaching and sponsorship.

What is Mentorship?

Let's start by becoming clear about what mentorship is and what it means to be a mentor.

Mentorship is a relationship between two people, often within an organization or association. The mentor and mentee are often in the same field or industry or sharing similar experiences. This relationship is generally developed on a no-cost basis.

In a workplace setting, a mentor is an individual in the organization who has desirable skills, knowledge or attributes that they can share with employees seeking broader business knowledge or career development.

The mentor has extensive business knowledge or functional expertise in one area or several, and is technically proficient in those areas. The mentor acts as a guide to the mentee to emulate or avoid specific actions or behaviours as a result of experience and learning. In short, a mentor is someone who has been where the mentee wants to go.

The mentor and mentee work closely together to discover and enhance acknowledged areas of development. This may be accomplished through a combination of learning opportunities such as meetings, job shadowing, counselling, tutoring or role modelling. It might also include selected and appropriate exposure and introductions to business or industry contacts. The premise is that the mentor provides the mentee with information or knowledge to which they would not normally have access.

It's important to understand that while mentors share their experience with a mentee and guide the mentee towards making decisions, it is the mentee who generally takes the lead in goal-setting. The mentee accepts the responsibility for driving the outcomes and steering the relationship. I've had relationships with mentees who did not take ownership, as have others whom I interviewed, and the results were less than optimal.

Sometimes mentorship will have different meanings, depending on the person's lens. Take, for example, George Gets, who worked at one of the top global accounting and consulting firms. George believes mentees need to take charge of their own goals, especially in a traditional mentorship where the mentor has years of knowledge and experience. The mentor is there to support and guide and while both benefit and learn together, ultimately the mentee needs to know where they want to go.

For mentorship to be successful there has to be the right energy between the mentor and mentee, the right vibration as he says. George has some other valuable advice related to coaching, and his life changes, before dying and after dying, that I'll share later.

A mentor typically has some type of experiential knowledge that will help the mentee achieve success. They can help navigate tough decisions, guide professional growth, share tips and expertise relevant to the chosen career or life goals. A mentor gives advice and support specifically aligned to the industry, role or organization, and again without cost.

Often there are a limited number of mentors within an organization, so many are now approaching "professional" mentors. I believe, however, that since mentors should not come at a financial cost, these individuals are not traditional mentors, but usually coaches, educators or consultants.

So where have all the mentors gone?

In the past, mentorship was found in guru-disciple traditions practiced in Hinduism, Buddhism, Rabbinical Judaism and Christianity, as well as apprenticeship under the medieval guild system. Many of these hierarchical institutions were male-dominated, and so it's questionable whether they work in today's business or academic worlds.

Is traditional mentorship a thing of the past, then, because it was a male version? Is modern mentorship the way of the future—and if so, what is it?

We shall see!

My definition of modern mentorship is one where every person has a mentor so they can learn and grow and in turn give back to others. Modern mentorship is everyday mentorship where mentor moments are part of all aspects of life and work. It's what Mentor Canada refers to as a mentoring mindset and I like to refer to it as everyday mentor moments.[3]

Mainstream business books adopted the lexicon of mentorship and sponsorship and coaching as ways to achieve career success, but this all remains in a predominantly hierarchical and institutional setting.

In 1970 these terms were not even in the general American vocabulary, and it took until the mid-1990s for them to become part of everyday speech. So where does that leave us today, 30 years later?

While much of the focus is the United States, mentorship has been embraced in Europe, as well as Australia and other countries, and it is continuing to grow today. Five years ago, when I started researching mentorship studies and business cases, and interviewing people about their mentor experiences, there were about a dozen well-known mentor technology platforms. Today there are at least 40 or 50 in the competitive marketplace of mentorship, a growing multi-million dollar industry.

Here in Canada, we are often lagging when it comes to mentor programs within organizations and in the non-profit volunteerism space—as in other people or talent development programs in the workplace. But change is happening even as I write this, which is very exciting!

While highly visible influencers such as Oprah Winfrey and Simon Sinek attribute their success in large part to having mentors, the same can be said for many less famous individuals. Whether as a direct teacher or simply inspiring others to become better versions of themselves, mentors impart the knowledge and experience they have gained throughout their lives.

When to Use a Mentor or Mentor Program

Everyone should have a mentor—always! Being mentored by someone truly is an opportunity and a gift. A gift of time and a gift of knowledge.

Organizations can leverage mentorship to build high-performance teams, and to help create heart-centered cultures, since giving becomes a part of the core values. If leaders and others with specialized knowledge are providing mentorship, the entire organization and all people within it benefit. This has a ripple effect on how people work with customers, in the community and the world (linking to corporate social responsibility).

Mentors should be part of the "DNA" of the company. Here are a few ways individuals within an organization can be supported by a mentor:

- During onboarding, a mentor can act as a "buddy" who guides the new employee for the first three to six months. This can increase the employee's comfort level in the job, which is likely to lead to better performance.
- When onboarding is complete, new employees could be paired up with mentors, and this can be an ongoing requirement of more experienced roles.
- Sometimes an employee needs to develop a specific skill set that is outside the scope of the manager, such as communication, finance, marketing, emotional intelligence, etc. This is an ideal time to use a mentor who has these skills and experience.
- A mentoring relationship can help facilitate the exchange of knowledge among peers (peer-to-peer mentorship).
- When a career change is desired, either by the employee or the organization, a mentor can relieve the uncertainty and help the person make the change successfully for all concerned.

- Sometimes a person becomes "stuck" in their career and doesn't know which way to turn. A mentor can help them become "unstuck."
- When someone simply needs a confidante or a connection to lift their spirits, a mentor is often the answer.

In short, a mentor can be a lifesaver in many circumstances, which is why I recommend having one—always and forever!

While the focus of this book is on mentorship, there are other relationships that are important to career and personal growth for employees that differ from mentorship. Let's now review two other relationships in the workplace with huge industry growth—coaching and sponsorship.

What Is Coaching?

While you will often hear paid coaches call themselves mentors, there are key differences, which I'll help unravel for you.

As I mentioned earlier, a mentor is not paid. Whether within an organization or another traditional volunteer mentor program, the mentor receives no payment for being a mentor. So, when a person is charging a fee to provide support services, they are probably a coach, educator or consultant. While a coach may from time to time put on a mentor hat because they have lived experience they can share, coaching is not a form of traditional mentorship.

I've worked with coaches, coach others and have also studied coaching. One of my professors, Haesun Moon at the University of Toronto's brief coaching course said that as she researched the world of coaching she found over 100 definitions, so let's just say even in that field there is a lot to sort out.

Here though we can look at some key differences between coaching and mentorship.

A coach is generally one who is guiding others to find the answers within. When one thinks of a coach, often what comes to mind is an athletic coach, but there are coaches in every industry from a life coach to a business coach to a financial coach—you can now pay for coaching in every aspect of life and career. Keep that in mind, as payment is a key difference between coaches and mentors.

The Merriam Webster Dictionary defines a coach as follows:

a: a private tutor

hired a *coach* to help her daughter prepare for the test

b: one who instructs or trains

an acting *coach*

a birth *coach*

especially: one who instructs players in the fundamentals of a sport and directs team strategy

a football *coach*

a gymnastics *coach*

While there may be some overlap between mentors and coaches, here are a few of the most common areas where hiring a coach can help one develop:

- Career choices
- Business acumen
- Entrepreneurship
- Skills development
- Fitness training
- Diet or nutrition
- Personal growth
- Positive self-talk or emotional growth
- Effective communication
- Relationships
- Parenting
- Smoking cessation
- Budgeting (stop wasting money or start saving)
- Home organization or cleaning
- Writing

As mentioned, there are life coaches and many more former executives, psychologists and professionals now starting niche coach businesses. The entrepreneurship world is booming into an entire self-development and coaching world and too much to go into in this book!

An athletic coach featured large in the life of Olympic athlete Sarah Wells. When Sarah was in high school a teacher told her she should try out for track and field. She had failed at every other sport, but it turned out she excelled at track and field! Sarah went on to compete at the highest level possible (a hurdler) and her original track and field coach, Dave Hunt, helped her get there. They stayed together for the next nine years until she made it to the Olympics!

This form of coaching is easy to wrap your head around, and it was in the 1980s that the coaching model started to evolve into other fields outside sports. The modern incarnation of coaching can trace its roots back to the Human Potential Movement of the 1960s, a decade of exploration in human growth and development.

Two eminent psychologists, Abraham Maslow and Carl Rogers, were champions of human potential and leading figures in the field of humanistic psychology. This movement promoted an optimistic view of human nature, stating that people had an inborn urge to achieve their full potential. As a result, the movement educated employers about the importance of treating people well, rather than focusing entirely on performance improvements. It's unfortunate that this still hasn't come to fruition, but there is further momentum today. The years of the COVID-19 pandemic focused us once again on bringing more humanity into the workplace. For more on the evolution of coaching, check out Humanistic Psychology.[4]

Remember there are times where someone may wear a coach hat, including a manager, or they may be a mentor as well.

Since the coaching boom, there is also a lot more focus on leaders or managers as coaches and these skills are definitely needed in today's modern workforce. Yet, I believe that creating mentor programs with mentors outside of the typical manager-employee relationship is one of the best ways to build a high performance, healthy and heart-centred culture.[5]

An effective manager-as-coach asks questions instead of providing answers, supports employees instead of judging them, and facilitates their development instead of dictating what has to be done.

Research from the Association for Talent Development (ATD) published in September 2020 showed that 90 percent of companies expect some portion of their managers to coach their employees, and 75% expect all of them to do so.

The coach may or may not have the technical expertise and/or the ability to do the actual job the coachee does. The coach's primary skill is the facilitation of internal learning, and it works best when they help the employee (or client) recognize and access their own strengths, knowledge and resources to achieve their performance goals.

Coaches use a variety of facilitation methods such as listening, questioning, reframing, reflecting and paraphrasing to help the employee "see and hear" what helps them be successful and what gets in their way.

Typical outcomes are that employees:

- Can identify their goals, gaps and action plans to achieve success
- Become more self-sufficient, resourceful and engaged
- Become conscious of the trends and patterns, behaviours or beliefs that support or detract from them performing to the best of their ability
- Feel empowered and confident in their abilities
- Make appropriate decisions and take appropriate risks that support their growth and learning
- Translate and reframe previous learning and experience into new situations, opportunities and challenges

Most coaches working with employees are paid and external to an organization, or there is a separate area within the organization with the expertise to coach. Many HR professionals are now also seeking certification with various coaching organizations recognized by the International Coaches Federation.

In addition, organizations are also trying to embed coaching skills into management competency as discussed above.

I interviewed several coaches as part of the research for this book, and it was interesting to me that even within the coaching community there is confusion about the difference between coaches and mentors.

One person I interviewed was Kristen Harcourt, a leadership coach who has helped executives and emerging leaders in organizations worldwide achieve extraordinary and sustainable results through increased self-awareness, emotional intelligence and mindfulness.

I like what Kristen had to say about this, as she had both mentors and coaches throughout her life and career. For her, mentoring is about sharing experiences and giving advice, while coaching is never giving advice. The coach's role is to ask powerful questions so that the person being coached has their own realizations and can make their own decisions.

Kristen believes that while consultants are problem solvers, a good coach is not solving an individual's problem, but helping them understand themselves. She did acknowledge that from time to time she may step into a mentoring role when she has a lived experience to share, and she does this with her client by advising them that she is taking her coach hat off and putting on her mentor hat.

I also interviewed Rosanne Carcasole, a certified coach with years of real-world business and coaching experience. She led teams, managed relationships and developed and implemented the strategies necessary to accelerate the success of brands including Coppertone and Dr. Scholl's, and now leads Rosanne Carcasole Coaching, which she founded in 2006. Rosanne was also aligned with the idea that a coach asks questions to help others come up with their ideas and conclusions, while a mentor gives advice and counsel, has theories or best practice experience from lived experiences.

George Gettas, whom I mentioned earlier, is also a coach. Here is what he shared: "As you know, I have two parts to my life—before dying and after dying. After the dying part I took it as a message from the cosmos as something still to do. I stumbled across coaching, and then I stumbled across coaching women." George views a coach as someone who helps others follow and find what lights them up through impactful question asking.

In a nutshell, then, my definition of a mentor does not include the exchange of money. Mentoring is something that should be freely given. You can have everyday mentor moments at any time, even in one interaction or meeting.

Coaches, on the other hand, are usually paid for their services, either by individuals or organizations. And coaches don't generally give advice.

I believe that both relationships are critical to an individual's growth; mentor programs and coaching programs are both important and budgets will determine when to use them.

Here are some ideas for using a coach or coach program in your organization.

When to use a coach or coaching program

Organizations should consider using coaches or coaching programs in several scenarios:

- **Leadership Development:** For developing leadership skills among high-potential employees or new leaders. Coaching can help them navigate leadership challenges, improve decision-making skills, and enhance their ability to lead teams effectively.
- **Performance Improvement:** To address specific performance issues with employees. Coaches can work one-on-one to identify areas of improvement, develop strategies to overcome challenges, and enhance overall

performance. This is the historic way that coaches were brought into organizations.

- **Career Development and Succession Planning:** Coaching can be instrumental in preparing employees for future roles and responsibilities, ensuring a smooth transition in succession planning.
- **Change Management:** During times of significant organizational change such as mergers, acquisitions, or strategic pivots. Coaches can assist employees and leaders in managing change effectively, reducing resistance, and improving adaptation to new processes or cultures.
- **Enhancing Team Dynamics:** To improve collaboration, communication, and conflict resolution within teams. Coaches can facilitate team-building activities and provide an outside perspective to help resolve internal team issues.
- **Supporting Employee Well-being and Resilience:** Especially in high-stress environments or during periods of organizational stress such as layoffs or economic downturns, coaching can support employee well-being and resilience.
- **Skill Development:** For specific skill enhancement, such as public speaking, time management, or technical skills relevant to the employee's role.
- **Diversity and Inclusion Initiatives:** To support diversity and inclusion efforts within the organization, coaching can help create a more inclusive culture and assist leaders in understanding and navigating diverse team dynamics.
- **Onboarding Senior Executives:** New senior executives can benefit from coaching to help them understand the organizational culture and dynamics, and to quickly become effective in their new roles.
- **Post-Training Reinforcement:** After significant training programs, coaches can help ensure that the learning is effectively applied in the workplace.

Organizations should evaluate their specific needs, objectives, and resources to determine when and how to best utilize coaching or coaching programs. It's also important to choose the right coaches--those who have relevant experience, credentials, and a good fit with the organization's culture

Now let's review the concept of sponsorship and how it differs from mentor relationships.

What Is Sponsorship?

When you think of the word *sponsor,* you probably associate it with companies that provide funding in return for advertising or their logo plastered all over some swag at a conference. That's not what we are exploring in the context of this book.

We are also not talking about the sponsor that someone might have as part of Alcoholics Anonymous, although many of the traits that make someone excel in this special role are likely found in sponsors in the workplace.

For our purposes, a sponsor relationship is generally one in which an executive or senior leader within an organization or similar role, uses strong influence to champion a protégé. (I use the word *protégé* here to differentiate from a mentee.) A sponsor can help the *protégé* obtain stretch or high-visibility assignments, promotions or other roles. The sponsor is putting their reputation on the line, so there is an expectation that the *protégé* will deliver excellence and be accountable for high-performance outcomes.

Sponsors are advocates in positions of authority who use their influence intentionally to help others advance, as opposed to only providing the advice, feedback or coaching offered by mentors. Both are important to advancement as employees navigate the workplace and earn growth opportunities.

A sponsor will actively help advance a career by advocating on behalf of the *protégé*. In doing so, the sponsor confers credibility on the *protégé*, and if the *protégé* doesn't deliver on expectations, this may reflect poorly on the sponsor's reputation.

I spoke with Greg de Koker, Co-Founder of a sponsorship app called Sandboxx. His view is that sponsorship helps accelerate leadership, engagement and inclusion, and he sees sponsorship as an advanced form of mentorship. It's when a senior leader (sponsor) is committed to the development and advancement of a *sponsoree*. It's also a two-way, mutually beneficial relationship between the sponsor and *sponsoree*. Please note this is the term used by Sandboxx and is the same as a *protégé*.

We talked about some of the key differences between sponsorship and mentorship.

A sponsor is someone who:

- Advocates for their sponsoree's growth and advancement
- Uses their reputation and social capital on behalf of their sponsoree
- Expects a great deal from their sponsoree,-specifically high performance and loyalty, as this is a two-way relationship
- Encourages their sponsoree to take risks and has their back
- Invests in the future of the sponsoree, the organization and themself

A mentor is someone who:

- May or may not work for the same company as their mentee
- Builds their mentee's confidence and provides a sounding board
- Offers empathy and an ear to their mentee
- Expects very little in return from their mentee, as this is typically a one-way relationship (hopefully it is also reciprocal)
- Focuses primarily on listening to, as well as advising, the mentee

I'd also add that the sponsor is in a position of power, and can open doors for the *protégé* in important ways, including:

- Increasing visibility by sharing the accomplishments of the *protégé* with other senior leaders and openly advocating for them in closed-door meetings. This is particularly critical in talent management meetings where important assignments and promotions are discussed.
- Sharing valuable insight. Sponsors use their unique perspective on the company to help their *protégés* identify and make strategic contributions that will increase their value to the organization and help them get noticed. Sponsors also provide valuable help in navigating organizational politics.
- Making meaningful introductions. Sponsors connect their *protégés* to influential and powerful people within their organization or industry who can help them advance.
- Candid Feedback. Sponsors can provide candid feedback to their *protégés* about their reputation in the organization and how they stack up against criteria for leadership.

Catalyst Research found that sponsorship programs resulted in more effective leaders and teams, as well as increased job satisfaction, commitment to the organization and desire to stay with the organization. They also strengthen the talent pipeline, bolster engagement, and improve company culture.

When to use a sponsorship program or find a sponsor

Sponsorship is one of the most effective ways to advance anyone in organizations—including high performers, high potential employees, new employees, women, minority groups, other under-represented groups—in fact, anyone.

Sponsorship helps employees feel included, valued, respected and empowered, which in turn drives employee engagement. Sponsorship also helps accelerate leadership, advancement and inclusion.

These benefits drive significant business results, such as:

- better corporate culture
- higher employee retention
- higher employee attraction
- better customer service
- higher customer loyalty
- higher productivity
- higher profitability

*Sponsoring Women to Success*h clarifies what sponsorship is—and isn't—based on the experiences of people well-positioned to provide answers: executives acting as sponsors and high-performing employees currently being sponsored. The report also presents data, practices, and articipant insights that provide actionable advice on how to foster sponsorship within organizations.

Analyses of interviews with 93 women and men participants revealed that sponsorship:

- is the key to advancing high performers and gives them greater opportunities to excel through skill development and increased visibility.
- acts as a differentiator at the top and a way of overcoming barriers for women.
- provides valuable benefits to sponsors, including feedback, enhanced skills, increased knowledge of company needs and opportunities, and personal and professional satisfaction.
- provides direct and indirect benefits to organizations, including better leaders and teams and increased organizational commitment.

What I've seen in other research is that for women, and historically disadvantaged groups of people, sponsorship is a key initiative that can enhance growth for these individuals. Since it's also arising in the equity, diversity and inclusion space, I think we'll have to monitor whether the model will show better outcomes than mentorship in the past.

Sponsors are expected to share their reputational and social capital, and leaders generally select colleagues and employees they know and trust and have worked with. This is because sponsors actively support and promote the advancement of those they take under their wings, as discussed in the MIT Sloan Management Review article, *Getting Representative Sponsorship Right in Your Organization*.[6]

The Sponsor Effect, by Sylvia Ann Hewlett[7] is an excellent resource for learning about sponsorship programs and the benefits associated with them. It is mainly for leaders who want to learn how to invest in others through sponsorship. Of particular interest Hewlett identifies seven steps to effective sponsorship for those interested in digging into this more.

I believe that mentorship can lead the way to future sponsorship, which is why I believe both programs are ideal in an organization. Once a mentor has worked with a mentee for some time, they may identify them as someone who they are willing to sponsor. So much can come from mentorship and this is part of the ripple effect that starts with mentoring with heart.

My Own Experience

I wish I had had a sponsor early in my career. I started my law career as an articling student at a mid-size Bay Street law firm. This was my first opportunity, and I was assigned a mentor. I remember him as a very kind man, but I don't have any recollection of him helping me navigate the politics of the firm and profession and finding my way around. I'm not even certain we had many meetings.

There were six articling students. I worked almost every day from 8 a.m. to midnight, saying yes to everything, not realizing the better thing to do was to choose wisely, or find a partner to help me say no. I didn't know what to do.

I understand now I should have asked more of my mentor, but what did I know? I was the child of immigrant parents from Poland (via England) and the first one to go to university, so I didn't have anyone in the family who could guide me in the business world. As my mom said once, after six years of law school, I was making about $2/hour for all the hours I worked. She was probably right.

Two of my fellow articling students ended up working exclusively with a couple of the partners and started to say no to work from other lawyers, championed by the senior leaders they worked with. That meant that the four remaining students (myself included) took on all the grunt work and everything else. They had the benefit of sponsors within the organization, and who do you think was hired back? These two students, of course.

If I had had a sponsor as well as a mentor, it might have made a huge difference.

I wasn't bitter at the time or now, as I loved my experiences there but it was tough to look for work, and it did impact the ego some-what. I was a mature student when I started school and older when starting my law career in my late twenties, and it's only now looking back that I see the experience through another lens.

It all worked out in the end, and I do believe that the journey unfolds in mysterious ways. A few years later, I was hired back at that same law firm, and although I only stayed for a short period, I learned a lot from each of these experiences.

Sponsors, mentors, and coaches can all make a difference in how individuals advance through organizations, but there are key differ-ences among them. Coaches provide guidance on development and often help with technical and human skills, such as active listening. Mentors help their mentees navigate their career choices through formal or informal mentoring relationships which I will review and cover, as the book is mainly focused on these relationships. Sponsors use their influence or leadership status to advocate for the advance-ment of an individual.

There may be some people who oppose the idea of providing opportunities to only a few select people. I think we need to move beyond this until equality becomes a reality. While I believe everyone deserves a mentor, some individuals need support that goes beyond traditional mentorship in the form of sponsorship. Sponsor Effect: Canada, published in 2017, confirms that sponsorship efforts can lead to more inclusivity in organizations and more work is needed here. Ritu Bhasin, the co-author of the study is leading the way with her work.[8]

While sponsorship can address equity and inclusivity, mentorship for all can also make a huge impact. That is why opening up the ability for everyone to receive mentorship, no matter what role, what stage of their career until they leave the organization, makes sense.

"A mentor talks to you, a coach talks with you, and a sponsor talks about you."—*Catalyst as also quoted by George Gettas*[9]

To summarize these three main relationships in the workplace:

A **mentor** is a trusted advisor who gives a mentee guidance and advice, based on built-up past experiences and knowledge.

A **coach** asks questions to help the coachee find solutions within.

A **sponsor** is usually someone in a high level position in an organization who advocates on behalf of a protégé.

Now that we've looked at the "Big Three" supportive roles, let's take a look at a few more relationships and compare them to mentorship.

2

OTHER SUPPORTIVE
RELATIONSHIPS

"The greatest gift you can give to you is being the best you; the greatest gift you can give to the community or family is also being the best you."—*Tim Cork*

There are many people and relationships that may affect our careers as well as other aspects of our lives. We've just reviewed the "Big Three"—mentors, coaches and sponsors. Let's now consider a few other meaningful and supportive relationships you'll find in the workplace and community.

One of the reasons we want to explore other supportive relationships is to identify how they may differ from mentorship, and also for you to realize that you may find mentors in some of them.

What is a Manager?

When I was interviewing leaders and professionals as part of the research for this book, I was surprised by how many people felt that prior managers or bosses were mentors. It's true that at times, a manager may want to put on a mentor hat or a coach hat, but it is important to highlight that the role is unique.

The Merriam Webster dictionary defines a manager as:

a: a person who conducts business or household affairs
b-:a person whose work or profession is management
c (1) : a person who directs a team or athlete, the manager of a baseball team
(2) a student who in scholastic or collegiate sports supervises equipment and records under the supervision of a coach.

Sometimes the manager and mentor roles overlap, and employees may find themselves being mentored by managers. But a manager is not necessarily a mentor.

A manager, or in some cases a supervisor, has a greater degree of influence over the action the employee takes and impacts the outcome of employee performance. They might set tasks or objectives for the individual or they may develop these collaboratively. One thing that sets a manager apart from a mentor is that the manager expects the successful completion of objectives for the overall benefit of the project, team or organization.

It can benefit managers and supervisors to develop and use mentoring skills within the workplace. However, when mentoring an individual you also manage, it can be more challenging to remain objective and non-directive, and to ensure that the mentee drives the agenda.

Many managers with strong leadership skills will manage, mentor and coach their team members.

What is a Consultant?

Sometimes the consultant's role is also thrown into the mix with mentors, coaches and sponsors. How is a consultant different than a mentor?

The Oxford dictionary defines a consultant as "engaged in the business of giving expert advice to people working in a specific field."

In other words, a consultant is somebody who advises a specific group of people.

Doesn't that sound a lot like the role of a mentor? Not really. A key difference is that a consultant is paid, as in many large companies such as Deloitte or McKinsey. With the growth of the gig economy and freelancers, the independent contractor as a business is also growing. In the U.S. about 36% of workers are engaged in this form of work or service. According to McKinsey, fifty-eight million American adults identified as independent workers in 2022, which equals about 36% of the American workforce.[1]

As a comparator, the mentor will generally address many objectives identified by the mentee depending on the mentee's goals, while consultants typically have a specific type of expertise and come into an organization for specific projects vs one-on-one or group mentoring programs.

Consultants generally fall into one of the following categories: management, corporate or independent consulting.

- The first category is **management consulting**, which is what most people understand, as provided by large firms like McKinsey, Bain or large consulting arms of Deloitte, Price Waterhouse Coopers, etc. They are generally hired to help large organizations improve operations or strategies, or manage significant change.
- The second category is **corporate consulting**, which covers a massive spectrum of job descriptions and focuses. The term corporate consultancy describes firms and service providers who give professional, individualized advice to organizations for the purpose of optimizing their business activities. Most clients are from the private sector, but the number of clients from the non-profit and public sectors is growing.
- The third category is **independent consulting**. People who have developed expertise through their jobs will often decide to hang out their shingle as consultants. It

can be any type of expertise, and many new consultants have come on the scene thanks to the gig economy.

Consultants solve specific and tangible problems as part of an engagement or project, or they may help clients gather the resources to achieve their own goals. Their job is complete once they've accomplished this, unlike a mentor who is with the mentee for the longer term.

A consultant looks at the big picture, helping management find solutions for the organization. Mentors generally focus on individuals, helping mentees hone their skills through personal development.

Mentors are often career and personal development-oriented, internal to the organization, focusing on the mentee's growth and unpaid. I have heard of some mentor programs where mentors come in and are paid, but that is rare and likely in the form of consultants, trainers or independent contractors/coaches.

Despite some of these differences, all three types of consulting and mentorship also share some common elements: knowledge transfer, sharing expertise and experiences; guidance though the nature and specificity may vary; and professional development, as all can contribute to the professional growth of individuals or organizations.

While consulting in its various forms is more focused on solving specific business problems and improving organizational performance, mentorship is centered on long-term personal and professional development through guidance and support. The choice between these approaches depends on the specific needs, goals, and circumstances of the individual or organization seeking assistance.[2]

What is a Counsellor/Therapist?

It is important to understand that the roles we have been discussing, especially mentor, coach and sponsor, are generally not professionals trained to provide counselling advice. While some coaches may have other specific skills and credentials such as a psychology background, the counsellor/therapist role is unique.

Oxford defines a Counsellor as "a person who has been trained to advise people with problems, especially personal problems", e.g. a marriage guidance counsellor.

The British Association for Counselling (BAC) was the first professional association to adopt a definition of professional counselling. As early as 1986 it published the following definition:

Counselling is the skilled and principled use of relationships to facilitate self-knowledge, emotional acceptance and growth and the optimal development of personal resources. The overall aim is to provide an opportunity to work towards living more satisfyingly and resourcefully. Counselling relationships will vary according to need but may be concerned with developmental issues, addressing and resolving specific problems, making decisions, coping with crises, developing personal insights and knowledge, working through feelings of inner conflict or improving relationships with others.

Counselling as part of coaching is also emerging. Many coaches use healing and other somatic exercises or modalities as part of their practice. It's really important to be clear that in the workplace most relationships are not formed as counselling relationships. Managers, mentors and other support people should be able to identify when someone on their team needs to seek professional counselling or a therapist. If employees are in distress, showing signs of depression or anxiety or in some degree of personal turmoil, help them seek support. Often counselling is provided as part of an Employee and Family Assistance Program.

For this reason, a counsellor is very distinct from a mentor role or other relationships we've discussed. A mentor may understand when a person needs counselling, but they do not have the expertise to be the counsellor.

What is an Accountability Partner?

In the world of coaching, community and masterminds, many people pair up with someone they call an accountability partner. In the world of work, people often assume the manager is the accountability partner, since they act as the key point of contact for the delivery of outcomes and help each person carry out work tasks and monitor benchmarks in line with personal career objectives.

Having an experienced manager to report to can be beneficial for moving projects forward, but it misses some crucial benefits a peer-to-peer relationship might offer. The manager often has to oversee so many people and projects that important details are left out of conversations. New employees are often unsure of what they should and shouldn't share with senior management.

With an accountability partner, both parties are learning and carrying out similar tasks. The feedback loop is fast and effective. Perhaps your accountability partner is familiar with a role from a previous job or you're both just starting out, walking the same path and sharing the same experiences.

There is also the benefit of being able to teach each other. There is no hesitancy when asking questions and no shame in admitting you're having a hard time. Each individual can pull another up with their intellectual strengths and get help where needed.

Other situations call for accountability partners with varying work styles, such as partner colleagues who work in different sectors or areas of the organization. An IT professional or tech developer can learn from subject matter experts or product marketers. They can share their knowledge with each other.

An accountability partner is closely aligned to the concepts of peer-to-peer or reciprocal mentors in an organization and is generally an alternative to structured and formal traditional mentorship.

Find the right accountability partner to act as a sounding board and *confidant* so you can stay committed to goals and aspirations.

My Own Accountability Partners

During my time as part of the marketing team at ADP Canada, I was fortunate to meet Elizabeth Williams, an incredible colleague. As I reflect on our relationship, Elizabeth mentored me and taught me tons about marketing and communications. Together, we worked on a podcast, blogs and other projects, expanding the company's brand awareness as it moved beyond payroll into human resources technology and services.

I learned so much from Elizabeth as we discussed thought leadership, advertising and marketing, and so much more completely outside my initial skill set. She learned about the world of human resources and culture, people strategy and employment law from my expertise in these domains.

It was after we both left ADP Canada that we became accountability partners. We began meeting regularly as we built our respective businesses and checked in on each other. We became sounding boards for each other's ideas, created action plans and monitored our respective progress. We mutually agreed to be accountable to each other and provide objective insights to each other, as well as mentoring and coaching from time to time. We agreed to monthly feedback sessions (although these can be any duration—daily, weekly or monthly). We shared wins, talked through challenges and discussed our action items.

Another valued accountability partner I currently have is Karen Dean, a speaker, coach and author who specializes in resiliency and mental health. I first met Karen at a women's business coaching event in Toronto in the fall of 2019. Then we connected on a business retreat in Mexico in January 2020. We shared a room and bonded over our Calm meditation with Matthew McConaughey. "Well hello there..." if you know, you know! We were dreaming big about our new business ventures along with other amazing women led by incredible coach Eleanor Beaton!

Karen and I live in different parts of Canada but have stayed friends and most recently accountability partners for our respective books. I finally got this to the finish line because we met weekly to support one another on our book writing journeys and encouraging and challenging one another along the way.

Having accountability partners has enriched my life, and I consider each of these women mentors and coaches too—but mainly they help me kick my own butt!

Having an accountability partner is different from peer mentoring or coaching, although there are similarities. Neither is it the same as masterminds or group coaching sessions since there are only two accountability partners instead of groups of people. While it may seem similar to peer mentoring, a key difference is that experience levels may differ. Peer mentoring within an organization is generally for leaders or individual contributor at a similar level.

An accountability partner can be successful if you have a solid mutual trusting relationship as you get more personalised and focused help with goals. Accountability partners are underutilized in organizations and are potentially overlooked as a development alternative.

What is a Colleague/Peer?

You have colleagues or co-workers within your organization, and outside of your organization in your industry. Colleagues and co-workers are simply that. They may become friends and in some cases they may become mentors; often colleagues form peer-to-peer mentoring relationships when both parties agree to take it to that form.

We may share some of our frustrations or celebrations with our colleagues, yet we often hold back on digging deeper and seeking out feedback on our work. It's usually a bit more surface-level conversation to start with. You may have cross-functional relationships that help with breaking down silos and promote innovation.

We learn from our colleagues daily, and in some ways we are all everyday mentors. For purposes of this book and to clarify the various relationships, a traditional mentor is generally a leader, someone who advises based on specific expertise, or someone you can learn from. And that's why peer mentors are more common than we realize.

The ideal mentors are usually not involved in the mentee's day-to-day tasks and operations in their role.

A colleague, on the other hand, is someone you work with towards organisational goals. When we dive into peer-to-peer mentoring this colleague relationship may change.

What is a Friend?

Friendships come in many forms; some last a lifetime and some come and go. What starts as a collegial work relationship may turn into a new friendship arriving from shared interests, values or time spent together. My friend Lauren and I, for example, started as co-workers, became friends and mentored each other. Lauren feels that you need friendship to have a strong mentoring relationship.

It's important not to misunderstand the nature of the relationship or to make assumptions. If you are working with a mentor as part of a formal program at work or through another organization, you may start to feel appreciation and even affection for the mentor. It's something that may be long-lasting, but sometimes it may be for a specific reason or season in your life.

Much has been written about friends at work—since we spend so much time with people. I've had friends who are mentors, and mentors who have become friends.

These relationships may evolve or overlap and are all needed in our careers and lives. It is knowing what you need and when. Early on, a mentoring relationship might feel a lot like a friendship. After all, you may spend time together, enjoy the same hobbies or activities, and have a lot in common. And you are building trust together.

Now that we have reviewed some of the relationships in our work lives, and understand more about what mentorship is and how it differs from other relationships in the world of work, let's focus more closely on the world of mentoring.

3

STRUCTURE AND CATEGORIES OF MENTORSHIP

"A mentor is not a teacher, but an awakener."—Robert Frost

There are various categories of mentorship, and it's certainly not "one size fits all." I believe there are only two types of structure: informal and formal. Within these two, however, there are various categories of mentoring, some of which work better in certain circumstances than others. In this chapter, we'll review the structure and a number of these categories.

Organic Mentorship

Informal mentoring, which I also call organic mentoring, develops when two people meet at work, an event or other function, or somehow the Universe brings them together. The two participants form a natural connection, it progresses, and a mentoring relationship begins.

The participants may not even realize they are in a mentoring relationship until years later. Take my relationship with Nora, which I described in the introduction. I met Nora when I was a senior leader at CIBC, working on a project to bring the first company-owned backup childcare centre to Canada. I admired Nora for years for the work she did for families and on work-life integration (or what she coined "work-life harmony").

When I left the bank and started my own consulting business, Nora hired me as a consultant, my first freelance contract in my newly formed business. I was able to shadow Nora, sit in on meetings with her clients, and learn a great deal from her. I did a lot of the research, and back then there was a lot of manual filing and organization before days of Zoom, shared drives and newer technology. Years later I realized she was probably one of the first real mentors I had in my life. It happened organically, through our work together, yet we never called it mentoring at the time.

Organic or informal mentoring works when the two participants have a strong connection and are good with a "go with the flow" process. Some type of common bond or interest brings the two together, and a natural synergy is present. There isn't a need for written documentation or structure, although that might occur as well. The two participants aren't matched by a software system or forced into an arrangement. Instead, they are willing souls united by an objective that they agree upon, which evolves over time.

When it doesn't work

It won't work if there is any feeling that someone is being taken advantage of. It won't work if there is more effort on one side than the other. It won't work if there isn't any trust between the participants. In most cases organic mentorship starts because people genuinely like each other and there is a purpose for the relationship.

Structured Mentorship

In structured mentoring, sometimes known as formal mentoring, the mentor and mentee meet as part of a program, usually within a private or volunteer organization, where the mentor participants are *not* paid. As I discussed earlier in the book, this is a clear distinguishing factor of mentoring as a whole as compared to other forms of guidance and relationships such as coaching, managing or sponsoring.

When it works

Structured mentoring will only work if the key ingredients are present: connection, trust, goals, and a time-bound relationship. It works for people who like fixed guidelines and specific guidance.

In my research interviews, many people spoke about some of the forced programs they participated in, which were generally unsuccessful. While there are some benefits to having matching software in larger organizations, structured mentoring will only work when the other key factors are present.

When it doesn't work

Formal mentoring programs don't work if an organization is trying to match people with very different values. Also, if there are not enough mentors, then a structured program is limited. If that's the case you might have to look at some of the other types of mentoring I'll review later.

Many of the people I interviewed for this book had experience with mentoring, both formal and informal. One example is Jane Watson, a Senior Organizational Development leader and talent and culture executive, whom I met through a DisruptHR speaking event in Kitchener Waterloo.

Having experienced both structured and organic mentor relationships, Jane says you have to deliberately make time to form solid mentorship relationships. In her view, a mentor shares experiences and guidance—it's a knowledge transfer relationship. During her time as a volunteer with one of the Human Resources Professional Association (HRPA) chapters she participated in formal mentor relationships that were extremely valuable while also revamping the program on the committee. This was a structured program and hugely successful.

She also was involved in an organic mentorship during time working on a project on sexual harassment. This also involved knowledge sharing and problem solving with her mentor. She was excited and yet at times paralyzed and terrified. Investing in this project and having guidance was also extremely beneficial.

No matter the form of the mentoring relationship, formal or informal, the benefits can be outstanding. Let's move on to the various categories of mentor relationships.

Categories of Mentorship

While the form or structure of the relationship will be one of the two mentioned above, there are many categories of mentoring that can develop, either as part of a program or organically. Each of these might be present in an organization, and there are benefits to having many of them available. There are also pitfalls or challenges with each type as well. This will depend on the size of the organization and the purpose of the mentoring program.

Traditional Mentorship (Top-down)

Mentorship just keeps on growing. While mentorship is offered in many non-profit or entrepreneurial organizations, its growth in for-profit organizations is slower. Those who do have mentorship programs are mainly the largest global or multinational companies, many of which are part of the Fortune 500. In most cases, the predominant form of mentorship remains the traditional or top-down model.

A traditional mentor is a trusted counsellor or guide. HR.com defines mentoring as a relationship in which a trusted advisor guides and shares knowledge with another person who is seeking guidance and insights.

The historic definition came from the classic Greek story *The Odyssey*, when the friend of Odysseus was entrusted with the education of his son Telemachus, which I mentioned in the first chapter.

Before going into when it does or does not work, let's review a few examples of famous traditional mentorship relationships.

Plato and Socrates/Aristotle and Plato/Alexander the Great and Aristotle

Mentoring can be traced back to these three relationships, and likely the saying "mentor and be mentored" was applied in these relationships. I've often said the true definition of a mentor is one who gives wholeheartedly without expecting anything in return. This is my concept of mentor with heart. Understanding the power of giving guidance and celebrating the importance of such a relationship is the first step in creating the ripple effect and impact.

Socrates was a mentor to Plato, who then shared a great deal of what he learned from Socrates, first with Aristotle and through him with Alexander the Great. This type of passing the learning along is what makes mentoring such an important factor in creating change in the world.

As I mentioned earlier, mentor relationships have existed for centuries, and their power is indisputable, but there are also many modern examples.

Oprah Winfrey and Mrs. Duncan

Oprah Winfrey is one of the most inspiring individuals in popular culture—and I have a dream to meet her one day.

Through television, literature, and philanthropy, Oprah is not only an innovator, but an influencer. She has said some of this success can be attributed to her fourth grade teacher, Mrs. Duncan.

"One of the defining moments of my life came in the fourth grade, the year I was Mrs. Duncan's student," says Oprah. "What Mrs. Duncan did for me was to help me to not be afraid of being smart. She encouraged me to read, and she often stayed after school to work with me, helping me choose books and letting me help her grade papers."

The relationship Oprah had with Mrs. Duncan shows the importance mentoring has on young, impressionable minds.

Teachers are often the first mentors who come into our lives, and I once wrote about my Grade 3 teacher, Mrs. Anderson, in a blog post. I was afraid of my shadow back then, and she helped me see my gifts. The results didn't always last, and so other mentors arrived to lift me back up again. I'll talk more about the different hats mentors wear in Chapter 5, but one thing I've learned is that mentors can help you only when you believe in your own worth first.

Jenni Gibbons and Roberta Bondar

Jenni Gibbons is a Canadian woman astronaut who was recently named to the backup astronaut for Canada's return to the moon. She is hoping to travel into space, following in the footsteps of her role model Roberta Bondar. Jenni says that our parents are our guides into the world around us, and she was able to benefit from that. Not everyone has the parent role models, so often we look to teachers or others around us. She was inspired by role models like Roberta Bondar and the late Marc Garneau.

She said she learned most from people close to her—teachers, peers and professors who invested in her and really listened to what she wanted to study and encouraged her. Those are the types of teachers and people we need to be mentors. Being in the right environments is pivotal in shaping our values, and how we move forward in life.

Bill Gates and Warren Buffett

Besides being the co-founder and CEO of Microsoft, Bill Gates has made a name for himself as an influencer and philanthropist. Gates attributed to his mentor, Warren Buffett, the power of taking a complex idea and putting it in its simplest form for the benefit of others.

When he first met Buffett, Gates did not think he and the investment guru had anything in common, but Buffett inspired him and awakened his interest in philanthropy. It's a well known fact that Buffett lives relatively frugally, giving much of his wealth to charity.

When Bill and Melinda Gates were setting up their foundation, they turned to Buffett for advice.

"We talked a lot about the idea that philanthropy could be just as impactful in its own way as software had been," Gates wrote. "It turns out that Warren's brilliant way of looking at the world is just as useful in attacking poverty and disease as it is in building a business. He's one of a kind."

Buffett had his own mentor in his younger years, and his work with Gates is a way of passing on those lessons to the next generation —another chain of mentorship just like those ancient Greeks I mentioned before.[1]

Mentorships have helped numerous individuals succeed in more ways than one. Whether as a direct teacher or simply inspiring others to achieve greatness, mentors take it upon themselves to impart the knowledge and experience they have gained throughout their lives. And in many instances, the mentee in turn becomes a mentor.

To reiterate, a traditional mentoring relationship is one where a more experienced person takes an often "younger" person under their guidance. The wise old owl with the youngling, sharing insights and helping the owlet develop new skills and experience.

When it works

Traditional mentoring works when the mentor has knowledge, experience and skills that the mentee does not.

While I believe this type of mentorship remains important, I'd like to start getting the world away from the concept of age. Many millennials and Gen Zs dislike the notion that only a wise old person can be a mentor. That's why some of the new forms of mentoring have appeared. There is still a place for the traditional top-down form of mentoring, but it's inevitable that the mentor will also learn something, so it's not really one-way.

When it doesn't work

Traditional mentorship won't work if:

- There is no clear commitment or one person is more invested
- The objectives of the mentee aren't clear
- There is no connection or chemistry between the participants
- There is no clear timelines (unless organic)

Reverse Mentoring

The term "reverse mentoring" was first mentioned way back in 1999, when it was embraced by Jack Welch, CEO of General Electric. Newer employees, with their deeper understanding of technology, were paired with senior management, who learned from their younger partners.

Several Fortune 500 companies have championed reverse mentoring since that time. This happened over 20 years ago, and it remains relevant today. We are continually going to need to learn from newer generations, as they shape the workplace and the future of work.

This trend is beneficial for both parties. Executives are able to stay on the pulse of trends that are most important to the millennials, and now GenZs, the younger participant feels more connected and invested because they are contributing to the improvement of their company at the highest level.

According to Lindsay Pollak, Millennial Workplace Expert at The Hartford, the company has offered reverse mentoring, formally and informally.

"For example," says Pollak, "The Hartford's employee resource group for young professionals has held 'speed mentoring' in person and via Skype. Company events that are not part of a formal mentoring program can be opportunities for micro mentoring. I believe reverse mentoring is so effective because both sides of the relationship have an opportunity to learn and grow and to enjoy the feeling of helping someone else."

I agree with much that has been written about the negative effects of labelling in mentoring. For example, referring to juniors and seniors, or even millenials and GenZs, puts people in buckets, stereotyped by age or other definitions. Learning is more likely when people think of others as simply colleagues.

There has been some negativity about labelling types of mentoring, and I agree with one writer, Charles Goff-Deakin, that perhaps we should not be using labels, as it creates a form of discrimination and unconscious bias. In his article he took issue with the terminology of reverse mentoring and terms used in numerous articles such as "Juniors, Seniors, Old Dogs, Millennials." People are getting tired of being bucketed by age or group stereotypes. We can all learn from each other regardless of age or any other identity.[2]

"Barriers are being broken down," he says, "meaning those in higher positions can still learn from their colleagues, regardless of rank and age." That is why I believe most mentoring is reciprocal.

Finally, the word "reverse" implies that the knowledge exchange is moving in one direction, from lower to higher management or from young to old. The name, therefore, has the same limitation as traditional mentoring, which I mentioned earlier.

The concept of reverse mentoring is quite simple. What began as a way for younger, more tech-savvy workers to mentor executives on technology has been adapted to a multitude of topics between younger and older colleagues. In this case it is newer generations of workers teaching those that are of older demographics newer skills, including a range of topics from social media and technology use, to teaching how to meditate, and much in between.

I don't like the term "reverse mentoring" because the terminology suggests it can't really be mentoring if one is younger than the other, and so we had to invent a new term—reverse mentoring. Many companies remain fans of this type of mentoring relationship.

When it Works

Many organizations believe that reverse mentoring will continue to work if there are clear guidelines about the skills that are being taught. Remember the lyrics, "Every generation blames the one before," from Mike and the Mechanics? Well, reverse mentoring can take this out of the equation.

There is a place for newer workers to teach experienced generations what they have learned from their recent studies. For example, their buying patterns as customers is something that more experienced leaders might need to understand. As long as the "age" card isn't part of the discussion, this rings true. It will work when there are specific skills that need to be taught, and this is primarily in the area of technology.

When it Doesn't Work

Reverse mentoring can potentially damage organizations who are working hard on fostering an inclusive, multigenerational and open workforce. Any distinctions based on age or gender may be perceived as discriminatory to some. Also, there is a movement away from hierarchy, and for organizations who are trying to empower their employees and advocate more modern learning and development, practices like reverse mentoring may not land well. It also won't work if there isn't great communication or no commitment from all involved.

Even if there is skills transfer, a Vice President or upper-level manager may actually not be that much older than their mentee. Putting limits on mentorship relationships will not always work, as we can all learn from each other. Sometimes these arrangements create unconscious bias.

Arguably, putting either the label "traditional" or "reverse" on mentoring is based on an unconscious bias, an assumption that regular mentoring (i.e. not reversed) is only from colleagues who are older than their mentees. According to Welch, it is reversed when the mentor is younger or more junior than the mentee.

We need to be able to define reverse mentoring without relying on outdated assumptions. We can reinforce the notion that anyone can learn from anyone without using specific labels. I think the topic of no labels might be a future book!

The point of creating mentor relationships is that we all learn in different ways and can learn from anyone who has the information, guidance and perspective we need for a specific knowledge or skill gap. The intent here is to describe the various categories for you.

When we look at multi-generational workplaces, reverse mentoring is a great way to recognize that skills are not always simply bucketed by experience or age. We all have unique individual strengths, perspectives and skills to share with others so adding reverse mentoring programs can be wonderful way to create connection.

Peer-to-Peer Mentoring

What is a peer? That's the first thing we need to determine before having a peer-to-peer mentor relationship. A peer is one that is defined as "of equal standing" according to Merriam Dictionary, or by the Cambridge Dictionary as "a person who is the same age or has the same social position or the same abilities as other people in a group." We don't want to get into the age argument again, so the best definition is one where in a work setting the individuals are at the same level or skill set.

Peer-to-peer mentoring can be described as a form of mentorship that takes place between a person who is an expert in a particular skill and a person who wants to learn that skill, where both the mentor and mentee may be at the same level in an organization.[3]

Peer mentoring offers a valuable source of support and information to less experienced team members who work within similar work environments, and can offer an organization or research team a low-cost method of training new research staff.[4]

When it works

It works when you have two peers who have something unique to offer each other and they both can benefit from the mentorship. Peer mentoring can also be beneficial within lean teams, for backing each other up (learning part of the other person's role when they may be on vacation, etc.). It works when people want to expand their knowledge in an area in which they haven't had a lot of hands-on experience, and are also willing to help others grow. All other factors that make mentoring meaningful must also be present.

When it doesn't work

It won't work if it is a competitive environment, where everyone is trying to get ahead, or if employees don't have anything unique to offer each other. If that's the case, your culture might be toxic as well. It won't work if there isn't buy-in from the organizational leaders (and that applies to most types of mentorship).

Reciprocal Mentorship

My favourite type of mentoring is reciprocal mentoring, and I'd argue that almost every mentor relationship could likely be a reciprocal one where each of the participants learns from the other. Sometimes it may not start out like that, but it's inevitable. We can learn from everyone. When I interviewed Lisa Fain, the Founder of Center for Excellence in Mentoring, she said that all mentor relationships require reciprocity in order to be successful. I agree with this and believe, regardless of the type of mentoring, it is generally true. Lisa said she believes that both the mentor and mentee give something to the relationship and both benefit in the partnership. For both of us the ideal mentorship relationship is reciprocal.

Reciprocal mentoring means that each participant will share their knowledge and skills with the other, regardless of age or level in the organization. Typically, this may mean pairing someone who is tech-savvy or has a good understanding of social media with someone with leadership skills or financial acumen. The point is there is two-way learning and growth as a result of the relationship. This is intentional matching of pairs who have something unique to offer each other in the way of technical or people skills.

In reciprocal mentoring, sometimes known as "co-mentoring", two people work together through a mentoring process in which they both take on the roles of mentor and mentee. This could be done by each participating in both roles, or by each person taking a primary role as mentor or mentee, but being willing to exchange roles from time to time.

As Hershatter and Epstein noted in their excellent paper about millennials[5] this generation expects constant feedback, mostly positive, and were raised in an inclusive era very different from their parents, the baby boomers. They are comfortable with a reciprocal mentoring relationship in which they share their accumulated knowledge and teach someone in a different generation.

Senior members of management taking the time to invest in working closely with their junior colleagues on projects that can be high profile can impact a career enormously. The pairing of unlikely individuals can result in positive results not envisioned at the start.

In the "developmental" model of mentoring[6], both parties go into the relationship expecting to be changed and to grow. In these strong alliances, reciprocal mentoring can happen spontaneously, as sometimes the mentee takes on the role of mentor. In these cases, it will work only if the mentee has received some of the training usually given only to mentors, such as active listening, challenging and asking powerful questions.

Reciprocal mentoring is definitely part of the future of work and is expected by newer generations to the workplace.

When it works

When everyone buys into the approach, when both sides have been prepared or educated on the roles and are committed to it, it will work. Reciprocal mentorship as a formal program will be successful if mentees are provided guidance on how to be excellent mentors, and vice versa traditional mentors can take a step back as leaders and be open to learning.

When it doesn't work

If one personality is too strong, or if one side isn't willing to share knowledge or have a give and receive mentality, it won't work. When any of the participants lets their ego get in the way, it won't work.

Mentor Circles

A mentor circle is an example of peer-to-peer mentoring, but applied in a group setting instead of one-on-one relationships. Mentoring circles were first made popular by Sheryl Sandberg, author of *Lean In* and former COO of Facebook. The group mentoring circle programs enable employees to find colleagues within an organization who share common learning objectives or interests.

Circle members (ideally between five and eight people) choose a topic—whether it be personal or professional—for group discussion, which is led by a circle leader. The leadership role rotates within the group, which has the additional impact of helping them build confidence and improve their leadership skills.

According to Catalyst, 65% of women who have been mentored will go on to become mentors themselves, thus continuously refilling the mentor pool and perpetuating the positive mentorship cycle for women.

A circle program can serve various groups such as working moms, women in leadership, minority women in finance, women in STEM and more. The circles can be gender specific or coed, depending on the program's intentions. This is a modern form of mentoring that can help employees feel more connected and engaged. I also believe mentor circles can be linked to employee resource groups or equity, diversity, inclusion and belonging initiatives in the organization. Safe spaces where peers can share their perspectives in a psychologically safe environment.

Mentor Circles were created at IBM, along with other traditional mentor programs according to Noreen Reid who mentored hundreds of newer employees in the technology industry throughout her career. While Noreen was not part of any of the mentor circles, she appreciated that it was offered. She also saw a similar commitment at Deloitte where she continues to mentor and sees the benefit of having circles of peers learn together.

Similarly at ADP Canada, one of my leaders and someone I interviewed for the book, Virginia Bailey, shared her experience with mentor circles. The circles were sponsored by Virginia and the head of HR at the time, and in many cases the members of the circle; co-facilitated the sessions. There were a number of focused sessions on specific skills-building topics as well as time to workshop situations on teams in a confidential collaborative setting.

A great example of a mentor circle is where one executive mentor will lead a group of five to eight mid-level leaders across different business functions. They might meet monthly, and a topic is chosen for a group discussion that engages the circle members.

The discussions are generally led by a circle leader, the executive or mentor (or as in the ADP case there were two executives who alternated leadership.) At other times the circle leadership might be rotated among the group, giving all members an opportunity to improve leadership skills, build confidence and engage in active facilitation for career development.

The Circle Way is also a way to facilitate group mentoring (or other meetings). It started years ago to allow everyone to be a leader, putting all in a circle of chairs vs hierarchical modes of power structure in boardrooms and organizations. It has evolved now with our focus on equity, diversity and inclusion. *The Circle Way* is an effective way to organize mentor circles and these practices can be incorporated online as well. Everyone has a seat at the table, and it is round not hierarchical.[7]

Circles can be expanded to those not in leadership roles, adopting some of the benefits of peer mentoring but instead of a one-on-one relationship it is a one-to-many. This expands the reach of the available mentorship and is much more time efficient. Mentor circles can also be hugely beneficial to enhance your diversity and inclusion initiatives.

When it works

Mentor circles work when the following best practices are in place:

- Have a limited number of participants (not too large to allow all to contribute)

- Identify purpose of circles (can have several different ones), communicate out to seek participants and identify the executive or leader
- Have someone designated to administer the program
- Develop and publicize goals for the program
- Set expectations for timing:
  - How long the program is (6, 8 or 12 months?)
  - How often you will meet (1X/month?)
  - Purpose (the why)

When it doesn't work

Circles won't work if they are not structured, or are simply a get-together to complain.

They also won't work if the leader is ineffective. If there are one or two dominant participants who take over meetings, this will create animosity. It won't work if everyone does not benefit equally and is included in the conversations and learning experience. Confidentiality must be maintained, so any breach of this will negatively impact the outcomes.

Without organizational buy-in, proper structure, or the ability to scale a program with software or otherwise, well-intentioned mentoring circles can hurt more than they help. As a 2011 Corporate Leadership Council report[8] found, only 36% of employees are effective at peer mentoring when left to their own devices, and only 7% of organizations focus engagement initiatives on improving these interactions. Mentoring is not something that always comes naturally to people, and unprepared participants can lead to inefficient programs that can become more of a liability than a solution.

Group Mentoring

At first glance they may look the same, but mentor circles and group mentoring are slightly different.

Group mentoring, as defined by Beth N. Carvin, CEO of Nobscot Corporation, is a methodology for individual development that utilizes multiple experts and multiple learners in a group setting. Although structured as a group, learning is individual, and each mentee works on their own unique learning needs and development goals.

The benefit of group mentoring is skills alignment. Mentees are able to pair up with experts in the area in which they want to improve. For example, a new young working mother will benefit more from an older experienced working mother who has been through similar life events than she would from a single male mentor.

Someone can actually seek out a mentor of their own age who has specific focus on a particular area such as technology, social media, or Excel skills, that he or she wants to acquire.

Although group members may be gathered in the same place, it is not the same as classroom training, because the mentees are driving the relationship. All the mentees follow their own learning and developmental goals, regardless of those of the other mentees in the group. Mentors ask questions, share relevant stories, and complete learning activities.

It can be useful for teams to have their own mentoring group when they have similar goals. They can use a variety of mentors of whom they can ask questions and reflect on the answers. Mentor and mentees can also share stories.

Peers can mentor one another in self-directed mentoring groups, or a trained facilitator can facilitate the discussions and support the mentees as they work on their goals.[9]

When it works

It works when participants feel uncomfortable in a one-on-one setting and they find group mentoring less intimidating. Mentees also get a variety of perspectives at the same time, as several mentors_are available to them all. They also get a richer, more complex understanding of whatever issues they are trying to resolve.

Group mentoring can help mentees build their networks, as they can build relationships with several mentors, as well as their peers in the group. Many mentees also enjoy the camaraderie of being part of a group.

Mentors can also benefit from group mentoring, as it can increase their influence without necessarily taking more time from their busy schedules. It can also help develop their communication skills—always a benefit for anyone in any position.

When it doesn't work

Similar to circles, group mentoring won't work if they are not structured, or simply a get-together to complain.

Group mentoring, like other forms of learning and development, won't be successful if the person facilitating them isn't skilled. There are always multiple personalities, so ground rules need to be set in advance. The other points made above are also relevant, especially the confidentiality focus. Groups are definitely much harder to manage and create collaborative spaces when juggling many personalities.

Micro Mentoring

Micro-mentoring is just what it sounds like: a short-term mentoring relationship. It might last weeks, days or even just a few hours, but there is no long-term commitment.

Lindsay Pollak, Millennial Workplace Expert at The Hartford, is a strong believer in developing young employees through mentoring, including micro mentoring.

"Micro mentoring is smaller, more informal opportunities for mentoring," says Pollak. "Social media creates opportunities for more micro mentoring, in that you can reach out via Twitter or LinkedIn to someone with more experience or expertise in a certain area."

Micro mentoring has become popular among millennials, both because of the availability of communication technology and their own more informal and casual nature.

By using micro mentoring, an employee may have multiple mentors over a shorter time frame, and can approach different people for areas such as job searching, interviewing, salary negotiation, onboarding, team development, and working with a new manager.

Micro-mentoring opportunities can take a number of forms. Below are two of the most common and easiest to execute.

Conference buddies

Colleagues often naturally attend conferences together, so it could be beneficial for your organization to pair up specific people for mentoring just at that event. You might even ask participants as part of the registration process whether they would be interested in being mentors or mentees for the event.

I have seen this approach used in my work with trade associations or membership-based organizations such as the Canadian Media Producers Association and the Human Resources Professional Association. Conference buddies, speed mentoring, or standalone mentor events are a great way to engage members/attendees.

Standalone mentoring events

Standalone mentoring events can take the form of speed mentoring, information exchange or brain dates. Ask your members or clients/attendees to express interest either serving as a mentor or being paired with a mentor. You can do the pairing through mini-events that go beyond simply facilitated networking.

For the dedicated time (one hour or 90 minutes), the mentees pick the mentors' brains a little, possibly asking for advice and a little professional guidance. One of the individuals I interviewed offers this type of mentoring in exchange for lunch. "Buy me lunch and pick my brain." He has mentored hundreds of individuals this way.

Sometimes someone just needs some timely advice but not a lengthy mentor relationship. Other times more is needed. So if you want to meet with Joseph Ranseth, give him a call (or better yet buy his book *Start a Movement* and you'll get some advice there). Joseph is a generous mentor who has also given his time to Big Brothers and Sisters and Futurpreneur as a mentor.

Not everyone is a fan of the "Can I pick your brain?" question, but really as we progress in life and our careers, there is beauty in the giving back through mentorship. It's why I call it mentoring with heart, we all have something to give to those coming up behind us.

With standalone mentoring, once the event is over, that's it. The attendees could exchange business cards and stay in touch as they could at any other networking event. And often this is how longer mentor relationships might form.

While this book focuses primarily on mentoring within large organizations, there is also a place for various types of mentors for entrepreneurs and small business owners.

Business Mentorship

In this digital age there are hundreds of freelancers and small businesses providing a myriad of services, and it seems everyone says they offer coaching or mentoring services. How the heck is anyone supposed to figure this sh*t out? I'm a coach. I'm a mentor. I'm both. What's the difference? I hope to shed some light on this confusion with this book.

"Pay me some money and I will reveal the 7 secrets to becoming a millionaire."

Although it is clearly ridiculous when stated like this, that is the general offer made by many so-called business mentors or coaches. People need to be cautious when wading through this. Remember what I said at the beginning—a traditional mentor is one who gives time and advice *for free*. They give and mentor with heart.

If you feel you want ongoing wisdom to help make your business a success, you may need a business coach or consultant, and often a mentor. It's fine to start with the information that's freely available online, but a good business mentor will pick up where that leaves off.

This person is someone with more business experience than you, from whose experience you can learn over time. In other words, you learn from their mistakes as well as their successes.

[10]Are you wondering why someone would do this without charge? Often their main reason is a desire to give back to society through the impact they have on their mentees.

When it works

As you can tell above, true business mentorship is from someone who wants you to succeed and has the knowledge, skills and experience that you're seeking. You can also pay for the coaching or consulting and many coaches do "teach you", but if you're paying them, I argue that is not mentorship. It works when the business mentor is committed to your success as a new business owner or entrepreneur, there is mutual respect and trust, and all the things we talked about for other forms of mentorship.

When it doesn't work

Like the many forms of mentorship discussed, business mentorship won't work if both parties are only in it for themselves. One has to be respectful of time commitments, and be organized. I've had a few situations where I volunteered to be a business mentor and the mentees simply did not commit to meetings or were not clear on what support they needed. We all get "busy" in the work of running businesses but if you're not interested in learning from others than don't ask them until you're ready to go all in.

There are a number of business mentorship programs out there and incubators and they are beyond the scope of this book. Like anything in life, what you put in you receive back. If you're blessed to find a business mentor who wants you to success, you are on your way!

Self-Directed Mentorship

I have been part of a few self-directed (or self-managed) mentoring programs—one with Start Up Canada, Start Up Women using the technology platform Mentorly, and one with the Human Resources Professional Association using the technology platform MentorCity.

In most traditional mentor programs, there is a program manager who will help facilitate matches across the organization. In self-directed mentoring, mentors who are interested in participating will agree to add their names to the pool of mentors so that a mentee can then review them and make a choice.

The responsibility is in the hands of the mentee who initiates the process and asks for assistance from the mentors who volunteered. Many mentees already know what they are looking for, and this gives them opportunity to take the lead.

When it works

This type of program has been implemented within many academic settings, where students/mentees can participate in programs and choose mentors that match their course of studies and future career plans.

At organizations who are more entrepreneurial or have a culture that isn't as structured or don't have the resources to hire a program manager this can work.

Also, if there are many locations or offices scattered across geographies this might be a good option. This gives more opportunity to expand the mentor program to more employees. The overall corporate objectives don't necessarily need to drive the why of the mentor program itself so it becomes flexible.

I love what Yale University is doing with its FLY program (Future Leaders of Yale), and it includes mentorship as well as self-directed mentoring. This program takes the participants through a process including self-reflection, choosing a mentor, etc.

FLY offers a group mentorship program through where early career professionals can learn to lean into their careers. A series of panel discussions is offered throughout the year, exploring career development topics for FLY members. Featured guest mentors represent various areas and levels of experience from across Yale.

When it doesn't work

Without formal structure or limited oversight my view is that self-directed mentorship will not have as much impact. There can be mismatches more frequently and lack of commitment and clarity. Also, mentees may have trouble initiating the relationship due to lack of confidence.

If there isn't commitment, similar to other programs, then the self-matching won't work.

There are many other categories and types of mentoring available, including alumni mentoring, mastermind groups, board of directors, employer association programs and other mentor platforms and communities who may also have a fee-for-service models.

I've covered the main types in organizations and associations outside them, and the world of mentorship is growing. You can check out more about each of them at our resources on lifeworkswell.ca.

Next we are going to take a look at the various roles that mentors and mentees take on as part of mentorship pairings, no matter what type of mentor category you choose to implement.

4

CREATING A MENTOR CULTURE

"One of the most important aspects of mentoring is its inherent reciprocity. When reciprocity is present, both mentor and mentee fully engage in the relationship." —*Lisa Fain*

Is mentoring simply a trend or buzzword?

What is it used for? Is it for talent management, leadership development, knowledge transfer or succession planning? Can it be used for all of the above? Now that we have some understanding of the various categories of mentor programs available, we will explore some of these questions and more.

It's important to identify the need, aim, context and reasons why mentor programs might be put in place. You want people to develop and grow within your organization, and for that you may want to create a mentor culture.

Even though I believe strongly in the power of mentorship, it may not be for everyone and may not work for your organization. I'm guessing, though, that you're interested in creating a mentor program that works for your organization, or you wouldn't be reading this book.

Now that you know about the various types of helping roles available, and you know your culture, there are a few questions to ask yourself before thinking about a mentor program for your business, department, division or your entire organization.

Here are some questions to answer:

- How much does your organization encourage honest, transparent communication?
- Is feedback or feedforward part of your culture?
- Do your managers engage in ongoing and timely reviews with their teams?
- Do people feel connected to each other and the broader vision or purpose of their organization?
- Do employees feel psychologically safe in the workplace?
- Is trust part of the values or inherent in the environment?

If the answer to any of these questions is no, then no matter how valuable mentoring is, it won't work in that environment. We'll review the key ingredients for mentor programs later in the book, and trust is one of the fundamental requirements for success.

In my experience it's not unusual for a mentor program to be placed on somebody's desk simply because the person has ventured to suggest that the organization might introduce a mentor program, or because the competitors have one.

"Great idea," says the manager. "Do some research on it and put together a proposal for a program."

I've been there—it's your idea so you lead it.

And then the program starts, often creating a great amount of work for little return. Eventually it fizzles out due to lack of commitment, time, budget, consistency and—let me say it—adequate expertise.

Mentorship, like any other change management intervention, requires a great amount of effort, knowledge, ongoing review and monitoring. If you are planning to implement a mentor program, make sure you have dedicated resources and a budget to go with it. You may need the help of external consultants or facilitators, or technology support, at the beginning. Or you may have an HR or talent professional who has led successful mentor programs in prior companies. Everything can be figured out with some commitment and guidance (and leadership buy-in).

What you invest you will gain in longevity, momentum and tangible outcomes for your company and for yourself.

This should be a no-brainer, but actually it is quite common for companies to jump on the mentoring bandwagon without really knowing why.

Mentoring is not a fad. It is a time-honoured activity that has now taken on new meaning by being implemented in workplaces. Please do not start a mentoring program unless you are committed, clear and confident about what it will deliver to you, what you'll focus on and what needs it will help to address as you would do for any other investments or initiatives.

The fact that mentoring is considered a "soft" activity does not mean it will not deliver hard and tangible outcomes. I'd like to remove the expression "soft skills" from the vernacular in the organization and replace it with "human skills". Key performance indicators (KPIs) need to be set up from the beginning, for the program, the organization and the individuals taking part in it, whether mentors or mentees.

Have you engaged your team in deciding whether they have needs that could be met via a mentoring program? Because if you have not, be prepared for an uphill struggle in recruiting participants –both mentors and mentees.

While I believe everyone deserves a mentor, mentoring *en masse* does not always work, nor does mentoring "at all costs". Mentoring for the "chosen few" does not work either, as it creates inequity and can cause disengagement.

Mentorship has to be chosen and embraced by your employees. People need to be willing to mentor and be mentored and accept that at times this may mean challenges and feeling outside their comfort zone.

Mentoring needs to be understood as aspirational, inspirational and an excellent opportunity to learn outside the box in today's hectic workplace. People must feel committed to it and must show this in their behaviour whether they are acting as mentors or as mentees.

Not everyone is suitable to mentor or to be mentored. Mentoring relationships should never be forced on anyone, and in fact participant commitment to the program needs to be monitored regularly. Similar to the saying, "When the student is ready the teacher appears", the mentee needs to be ready and willing to commit and the right mentor will arrive.

I would like to say that mentoring in the workplace is a grassroots activity, but unfortunately it is not so. While organic or informal mentoring can work effectively, any mentoring initiative must be actively supported by the leadership and ideally must have a champion and/or sponsor in one or more leaders.

When the senior level of any organization believes in the value of mentoring, the message is shared out and reaches all levels, giving permission to dedicate time and resources to mentoring. It's ideal when C-suite executives act as mentors themselves and also are mentored by newer and early-stage employees through reverse mentoring. By role modeling mentorship, executives and senior leaders are actually reaching out to less experienced team members and proving that everyone can find time to help others develop and flourish.

One of the key success criteria in creating a mentor culture is to ensure that mentors understand the impact they can make. If they Mentor with Heart™. The ripple effect is real. Everyone is lifted up and will contribute more passionately and effectively and with positivity toward other team members, clients, their community and the world. Having the right skills to be highly effective mentors and mentees every day and as part of programs is going to make a huge impact.

In order for mentorship to be a success you also need mentors and mentees to understand their roles and responsibilities, and we're going to cover this in the next chapters.

5

ROLES AND RESPONSIBILITIES OF A MENTOR

"Strong mentorship relationships have a degree of give and take; it's what you're going to give to this relationship and not just what you're going to take."—*Michael Bungay Stanier*

If you do an online search for the word "mentor", you'll find numerous quotes and definitions. It seems more companies are focused on mentoring than ever before. It's about time!

You will also find mentor coaches, and those using the words "mentor" and "coach" interchangeably as I touched on earlier in Chapter 2. Sometimes the lines are blurred, and a mentor may wear different hats. Depending on the mentor's background, they may draw on a number of approaches such as teaching or coaching, or perhaps even counselling in some cases. Since the focus of this book is primarily on unpaid mentors, it might be helpful to dig a little deeper into the roles a mentor can adapt to as well as the various styles present in mentors.

One of the things I heard often when I interviewed leaders for this book was that they didn't know how to be a mentor. This was a bit of a surprise to me, as some of the organizations they worked at were around for ages, and the leaders were in business for years. It might go back to the broader challenge that leaders are often not taught these essential communication and relationship-building skills as part of academic programs or internal learning programs. The other issue that has always existed is that managers are often trained in the necessary technical competency before promotion, but not in people or human skills.

All managers need to learn how to be a mentor, coach or sponsor. There are some who are intuitive teachers, but those are very few. Many of the leaders I spoke to were part of large organizations without mentor programs to guide them, or the programs were underground and they didn't even know they existed. When they were approached to be a mentor, they were at a loss as to what to do.

If your organization plans to implement a mentor program, it's important to consider what types of guides or advisors are available. On a personal level, if you have been asked to *be* a mentor, consider what kind of mentor you want to be. It's also crucial that you have a roadmap to guide the process and discussions with your mentee.

While I believe wholeheartedly in the value of organic mentorship, in organizational programs you need resources and structure or you'll flounder, and that's where many of the relationships fail.

In an earlier chapter you met Elizabeth, my accountability partner *extraordinaire*! While at a large organization, she was approached by several individuals who asked her to mentor them. She said she would, but she realized there wasn't anything she could turn to as a guide. Then as she did some digging, she discovered that there was another "secret" mentoring program for the "chosen few." (This is an issue we'll explore later when speaking about communicating your programs.) The bottom line here is that although she is an amazing person with tons of knowledge, she had to learn and self-teach her way through to make sure the relationship was successful.

In Chapter 1, I identified the differences among mentors, coaches and sponsors and how these relationships are mainly applicable to organizations. Remember, for purposes of this book, I've defined a mentor as someone who is doing this out of the goodness of their heart, as a volunteer, or as part of a program within an organization where it is not their primary role (and they aren't paid for it).

While one of the main purposes of mentoring is developmental capability, it is also true that one of the best gifts a mentor can offer is to help their mentees discover their own wisdom as well, and work towards self-reliance and commitment. This can be accomplished through many different styles, depending on the individuals involved. And really it is all about being a Mentor with Heart™.

Philip Wilson, a mentor of mine and an incredible leader in the HR field, says being a wonderful mentor comes from doing it for the right reason. If you're being a mentor for advancement or accolades, it won't work. Do it because you care.

Let's take a look at the various roles or styles that mentors can bring to a mentorship relationship.

Mentor as Teacher

This is by far the most widely known role of the mentor. The mentor imparts knowledge, expertise and information, usually through discussion or explanation and instruction. The mentee may have sought out the specific mentor because they have some particular skills or expertise that the mentee needs to develop. It could be business acumen or financial knowledge transfer, or it could be non-technical needs like communication or people skills. (You may have noticed I am not saying "soft" skills, as this term undermines the value of emotional quotient (EQ) skills and I'll rant about that at another time.)

Reverse mentoring, in which technical social media skills from a newer employee are taught to senior executives, is a good example of the mentor as teacher. It's generally a one-way flow of information.

There is less engagement if the mentor is only playing the role of teacher without any insights or dialogue coming from the mentee. So when I think about the mentor as a teacher I think that everyone in the organization could likely step into this role for the strengths and zone of genius they operate in.

A teacher cares about the person they are learning with; they share their wisdom and pass it on freely.

Mentor as Connector

Sometimes people are approached to be a mentor because they have a huge network, and are known as connectors.

Many mentors are happy to open up their networks and help the mentee meet some key people to assist. They are naturals, and being a *Mentor with Heart*™ comes easily to them. But this should only occur once trust is established in the relationship and it is progressing well. A mentor who makes an introduction has their reputation on the line, and it's important not to be taken advantage of. Mentors who are connectors enjoy people and expanding their community to others, but some believe it has to be earned.

Sponsors are often big connectors who use their networks to champion the person they are advocating for.

One of the Gallup skills found in Strengthsfinder is Connectedness. I think many inspiring mentors likely have this strength and belief that they are part of something bigger, a collective, and for that reason mentors that are connectors believe in the unity of humankind, and build bridges for others.

A connector is considerate, caring and accepting, with strong values. They can open doors for their mentees.

Mentor as Supporter

> My mentor said, "Let's go do it," not "You go do it." How powerful it
> is when someone says "Let's!" — *Jim Rohn*

So much is being written today about finding your community, your *tribe* or other support system to help you through life, including career goals. One of the roles a mentor may play is that of a supporter or what many have called *cheerleader*. I've been studying language use recently, and perhaps it may be time to reconsider some of the connotations associated with certain words. I know many use the word *tribe*, but for me that belongs to indigenous peoples.

What does the word *cheerleader* conjure up for you? Be honest here! Is it a rah-rah young female doing flips with a mini-skirt and tight top like the Dallas Cowboy cheerleaders? Well if that's it, then maybe we should change that vision.

Or maybe not. Maybe that's exactly who you need in your corner. Someone who will literally do back-flips for you and help you celebrate your wins, even the small ones!

The *Oxford Dictionary* defines a cheerleader as:

a member of a team that performs organized cheering, chanting, and dancing in support of a sports team.

Or for our purposes, here:

an enthusiastic and vocal supporter of someone or something.

I'm not sure I see my colleague and friend George Gettas (whom you met earlier) as a Dallas Cowboys type of cheerleader, but he definitely cheers on all of his clients, as well as women in the world.

The mentor as supporter is one who will happily cheer us on, regardless of gender identity. We have probably had these supporters throughout our lives. I also see them as similar to the champions or sponsors I talked about in Chapter 1.

The world is filled with shared stories now that we have social media and a wide ability to spread our voices, and the word "mentor" is thrown around a bit carelessly. Why is it that so many stories I read about are those of negativity or bullying and the impact that words or even physical threats had on us? Everywhere I turn now, I hear someone overcoming not being good enough or put down by others or deeply wounded or hurt. I'm not minimizing any of that impact. What I am saying is it's unfortunate we don't hear more about the person who lifted us up, those Everyday Mentors™ that I wrote about in one of my blog posts.[1]

It's definitely time that mentors took on the role of supporter. The leaders who understand this are those who demonstrate the importance of positive reinforcement or kindness, and yes, direct feedback delivered in a kind way. These are the ones that mentees remember. The mentors who help guide an individual to find their way, their worth, to find their voice, their identity and simply be themselves.

Having a supporter as a mentor will help create a strong relationship and build trust more than a critic or challenger—even though those roles might be important at some point as well.

Mentor as Challenger

I know I just finished saying you must have a number one fan in a mentor to be successful. I think sometimes, though, we need "tough love".

A key role a mentor might play is helping their mentee navigate decision-making. It's important for a mentor to be able to provide this type of advice without being harsh. It's all in the delivery! Brené Brown's "clear is kind" concept is a good way to think about this. This is why communication skills are such a key attribute that effective mentors possess.

The role of the challenger is to be frank and honest about a bad decision or costly mistake that a mentee might be about to make. They may well need a mentor precisely to avoid making bad decisions!

Take for example, a young man who worked for one of my clients. He was looking for work and wasn't happy with his current arrangement and salary, even though he loved the company he worked for, and the people and industry. Since he didn't have a mentor, he accepted a job that was not really what he wanted to do, but that was offering more money.

He approached his current manager, who then wanted to retain him and sought my assistance. We were able to give him a raise as well as additional responsibility to help develop him.

Where was the mentorship and guidance that could have avoided this? He had already accepted the offer, which isn't a sign of good judgment, and could impact his reputation. In the end, he's happy, but if he had had a mentor to ask for advice, all of this could have been avoided or handled differently.

You might be lucky to have more than one mentor, and perhaps they play various roles, like the "good-cop/bad-cop" we all know about from the movies, or sometimes the mentor can play all of these roles when warranted.

Challengers will hold a mentee accountable as well, and so if a goal is set, then they will check in to see if the mentee is following through. Again, with the right relationship and chemistry, a mentor will understand that all of this will be part of the journey. The strong relationship, some trust and understanding is part of the mentoring experience.

A mentor in this type of role will make sure that ego is contained, and that various perspectives and approaches are considered in decision-making. Calling someone in takes a very unique skill that only some mentors have. We all have learning and growing to do, and this is part of a solid mentor relationship.

Helping mentors by giving them guidance and even training can go a long way to ensuring the mentor relationships are successful.

The challenger is your *tough love* mentor who is there to help shine a light on the gremlins you may be holding that get in your way.

Mentor as Coach

Some mentors are also coaches (or coach-like), and some coaches also call themselves mentors. And some managers are mentors and coaches or none of the above! No wonder it's confusing.

I once received an email from a woman I follow online to invite me into her mentoring program at a reduced rate as a Black Friday sale. These types of offers are available every day—"Come sign up for my Mastermind or my Coaching or Mentoring class".

This doesn't align with my interpretation and understanding of the role of a mentor at work and in the world. This is where I believe it is a disservice to the industry of coaching that everyone can claim to be a mentor or a coach, even though we have many institutions that certify coaching.

I have heard of some paid executive coaches who will figuratively take their coach hat off and put on a mentor hat when guiding their clients, and I mentioned this earlier when I talked about Kristen Harcourt's perspective.

In the world of work, the focus of coaching is usually task and performance, and that's why we often hear that a manager should also be a good coach.

As we discussed earlier, coaching is different from mentoring but some mentors can adopt a coach-like approach. This is another role a mentor can assume. You may not simply be giving advice or recommendations—you may have a natural ability to ask questions and let your mentee find their answers.

One of the coaching programs I recommend is *Stand Out,* run by The Marcus Buckingham Company (TMBC), where you focus on strengths. TMBC created an assessment that pinpoints your lead and secondary strength roles, as well as your combined role. This provides you with your comparative advantage to stand out at work.

This strengths-based assessment is different from the Character Strengths or StrengthsFinder 2.0 in that it measures what we do at work versus who we are at work. The *Stand Out* report gives you the definition of each strength role, how you are most powerful, phrases to describe yourself, how to make an immediate impact, how to take your performance to the next level and what to watch out for. You'll get an idea of your ideal career as well.

Coaching involves helping an individual use what they already know to solve the problems before them. Coaches generally ask questions and are trained and certified through organizations such as Co-active Training Institute or Adler Professional Coaching. A mentor generally has the expertise being sought and so often gives unsolicited advice, whereas a coach is trying to get the individual to find their own answers.

ICF Credential-holders are part of a self-regulating group of reputable coaches who provide accountability to clients and the coaching profession as a whole. They pursue and complete rigorous education and practice requirements that provide unquestioned legitimacy to their commitment to excellence in coaching.

So sometimes a mentor may play the role of coach to develop the individual without trying to impose their own personal values and beliefs on someone. A great mentor will likely take on all of these various roles, and wear all of these hats to help their mentee.

Mentor as Counsellor

When we spoke about the difference between a mentor and a counsellor, we looked at very specific counsellor designations such as psychologist, psychiatrist and similar professions. These counsellors are trained to address very important issues such as self-esteem, depression and other scientific diagnoses. Learning from professional counsellors, as explained, is generally a one-way learning experience where the counsellor helps someone deal with some difficult, and sometimes extremely traumatic, events in the person's life.

The mentor should not adopt these roles, but can help identify a need to refer to these professionals. The mentor can, however, use counsellor-like skills to listen and question the mentee to help them build self-confidence or self-awareness.

I highly recommend therapists early in life, outside the mentorship role. It's worth noting that if a mentor needs some help, it's crucial that they get it, as you can't help others without first dealing with your own internal self.

Mentor as Awakener

"A mentor is not a teacher, but an awakener." —*Robert Frost*

So what does this mean? When I think of an awakener, I think of that inspiring person everyone wants as their mentor!

Full transparency: I did not come up with this term "awakener", but I love Robert Frost's take on it and others who have reviewed it. Athena certainly awakened Telemachus through her role as Mentor.

This person is often someone who lights up a room or has an incredible energy that attracts everyone to them. Doesn't that mentor sound like the one most people would want in their corner? An awakener is someone who has an immense impact on the mentee and helps them transform.

There may be other styles and/or roles that come to mind and I'd love to hear your views in the future as the world evolves. Let's now take a look at the responsibilities of a mentor.

Responsibilities of a Mentor

Obviously the mentor needs to take this role seriously and commit to the relationship and supporting the mentee. This should not be taken lightly or as an afterthought.

If your mentor program forces people into the role, it is not going to work as there is no passion or excitement about it. The reason most people mentor is that they want to share, or they are natural born teachers and huge givers. There are, however, a number of responsibilities that should be clarified in a mentor program up front, and setting up those expectations at the outset is important.

Here are a few of the key responsibilities and expectations to include in your mentor guidance and training.

The Mentor:

- commits to the mentorship relationship for an agreed period of time
- collaborates with the mentee to establish explicit goals and objectives, and reviews them at certain milestones, and at the end of the relationship term
- takes initiative but allows the mentee to drive the process and take responsibility for their growth, development, and career planning

- commits to meeting with the mentee on a regular basis (during regular business hours) and at a minimum one hour per month
- provides a psychologically and physically safe space for open and honest dialogue
- actively listens to their mentee
- provides frank, honest, and constructive feedback
- provides encouragement and assists the mentee in identifying professional development activities and personal growth opportunities
- maintains confidentiality at all times, unless concerns have been identified that warrant referral to a health professional
- respects the mentee's limits and acknowledges their own limits
- recognizes and works through conflict in caring ways, invites discussion on differences with the mentee, and arranges for a third party to assist if necessary
- makes only positive or neutral comments about the mentee to others; if disagreement over behavior or values arise, differences are shared with the mentee; if necessary, takes steps to end the relationship and tries to find the mentee another mentor
- maintains a professional relationship, doesn't intrude into the mentee's personal life or expects to be close friends, unless that evolves naturally
- renews or ends the relationship at the agreed upon time, and
- keeps the manager apprised of mentoring activities if necessary

Skills and Qualities of a Mentor

When setting up your program and choosing mentors, there are certain personal characteristics and competencies to look for. Here's a list you can use as a quick reference as needed.

A great mentor is:

- able to teach
- committed to a learning exchange
- an excellent listener
- empathetic
- a rapport builder
- one who encourages dialogue
- self-aware
- understanding
- intuitive
- a source of expertise and wisdom
- observant
- a relationship builder, and
- one who asks questions well

Checklist for starting with a new mentee

For participants in your mentor program, you should have a mentor guide or checklist to help mentors prepare, along with education to help them succeed. Feel free to use the following checklist or adapt it to your needs. You can also find additional resources on the Life Works Well website.

Starting a mentoring relationship is a bit like hiring a new employee, and before committing with the mentee, the mentor should assess the fit. I suggest interviews for the benefit of both the mentor and mentee and the following are some questions that will help. You can check out the icebreakers in the website resources as well.

Before agreeing to the relationship, ask the mentee:

- What is the goal or objective that you'd like to focus on?
- How long do you think it will take to get there?
- How much time do you have to commit to this?

- Will you put in the time to be successful?
- What makes you think I'm the right person to mentor you?

Once agreement is established:

- How often do you want to meet?
- Do you want to meet in person, via video or via telephone? Or a combination of all three?
- What is the duration we need together—6 months? 1 year? Longer?
- Revisit the goals or objectives, and set agenda

Your program should include an agreement or commitment document to ensure accountability. This is often part of mentoring match-ups in formal programs both in private and non-profit organizations or associations. You can create something very simple to demonstrate the commitment, and if you have a mentor software platform it is usually in electronic form.

Futurpreneur is one example of an organization that helps new entrepreneurs through mentorship, as well as providing financial support to the ventures. As part of their program, mentors register and volunteer and provide a profile of their background so that mentees can be matched based on their needs. I have been mentoring with Futurpreneur since 2017, and have had several mentees throughout this time period.

Each relationship at Futurpreneur requires an 18-month commitment, and there were a number of tools to guide us along the way. We often started out with very regular meetings, and sometimes flexibility was built in. Some of the mentor pairings started right before the pandemic so it also involved one-off guidance. I was honoured to be nominated by two of my mentees in 2020 for the Mentor of the Year Award and was one of the top five finalists. While accolades aren't the reason I went into these mentorship relationships, it was a gratifying experience, and I encourage you to look for outside opportunities to mentor as well. This will start that ripple effect of mentorship for all that I have been emphasizing throughout this book.

For industry organizations that are creating these types of mentor programs, the mentees also receive funding in addition to mentorship. A word of caution though is that some of the entrepreneurs are more interested in the funding than the mentoring. If that is the case they are missing out on a wealth of knowledge if they don't take advantage of the mentorship provided.

There are mentor matching platforms that let you do this online. For example, I was Chapter Chair for Mentorship with the Human Resources Professional Association in Ontario, Canada, where we used a platform called MentorCity. I've provided an overview of some of the key platforms in the Resources section of the Life Works Well website.

It's important not only to set goals and objectives, but to have a system in place to measure the results.

When documenting the goals and objectives, clarity is key. Similar to setting up SMART goals for performance or development within an organization, setting up goals or objectives for the mentor relationship will ensure success. For example, it can be career-based in order to get to the people manager role in another department, or it can identify the skills needed to get a promotion within the mentee's team.

Measure progress using any tools provided, and check in frequently, and self-assessments can be developed as part of more formal programs.

Checklist to measure success

You will find more detailed checklists and guidance throughout the remaining chapters and the resource guide, along with a guide to various current vendors that mentor-match (for those that can afford it and have much larger organizations or budgets).

If it's an informal mentorship, you can still apply the same principles to ensure that there is some structure to the process. Now more than ever your data can open doors to huge business returns if utilized well. Be creative in the process, but show me the numbers! Or if you love the movie *Jerry MacGuire,* "Show me the Money!"

At a high level, here is what you can measure:

- **Engagement**
  - Is the mentee showing up on time, leading the way?
  - Did they show up to a kick-off event?
  - Are the meetings kept even if only once per month?
  - Is there good dialogue?
- **Individual Goal Tracking**—this is output oriented and can be measured. Similar to goals in a management-by-objectives organization, goals are tangible, e.g. finished a course to get certain credentials; met with five people to network; attended three industry events, etc.
  - Have the goals been met or not? Yes or no?
  - If it's a larger program, set metrics at outset of program —how many met goals? how many meetings? how many participants?
- **Organizational Goal Tracking**
  - Create macro level goals if you are implementing a mentor program in your organization. You need to be able to prove the business case to the Board of Directors or the Executive team and prove the return on investment. Organizational goals can include things such as increasing diversity at the management level, or increasing leadership development or succession planning; or as always, employee retention or promotion. In order to measure this accurately you'll need statistics and data prior to the implementation of the mentoring program.
- **Employee satisfaction**—you won't know if you don't ask. A little different from engagement, employee satisfaction can be accurately measured through surveys.

- How many people rate it as Excellent, Very Good, Poor, etc.? This data is extremely valuable for the future of your program.

Choosing Mentors for the Program

A good mentor can come in many forms, and isn't always the most successful star performer in the organization. A good mentor is someone who has a genuine commitment and desire to help in the development of others. The mentor must be willing to share their own lived experiences, successes and failures and be able to reflect on experiences.

The mentor must devote the energy, time and commitment to building the relationship. They must be willing to open up past experiences for learning opportunities–the good, the bad and the ugly.

A good mentor is an effective listener, and will create safe spaces for conversation. They will ask insightful and meaningful questions, and encourage self-reflection by the mentee.

Like any other corporate program, this is not just about ticking boxes. This is about making a real impact in employees' careers and experiences at your company.

If you are going to have someone helping with the matching process and looking to make this successful, take a look at the skills and qualities mentioned above when looking for the mentors for your programs.

Reporting and Program Success

If mentor relationships are so key to one's success, why don't organizations implement them more often?

Data and insight are great, but leaders need much more to be convinced, and they need the data and outputs to have meaning and impact on their bottom line. Sometimes this is acquired through technology, and analytics and data may come from this rather than manual surveys and spreadsheets. I provide more information on technology and program implementation in Chapter 7.

A mentor also has the responsibility to participate in giving feedback, answering surveys, providing qualitative and quantitative input to the program manager.

Surveys

Surveys can fill in the more qualitative gaps that analytics fail to uncover. Engagement and utilization analytics will only tell you part of the story. The complete story requires asking people how they are doing; how satisfied they are; and how the program could be better.

Mentors have a role in providing open and honest feedback on how the relationship is going, what's working and what's not so the program can be continuously enhanced.

Reports

Leaders love data, and reports and numbers that make sense. They also want these summarized and explained in an easy-to-understand and cohesive way. There are a number of ways to build informative reports. You can use your manually collected data to assemble reports yourself, or export and download accurate software-derived insights from mentoring software platforms.

In the 21st century of data analytics, being able to prove return on investment for your program should be easy. There are numerous ways to comfortably report on program engagement, employee satisfaction, employee development, and organisational goal attainment with ease. Show me the mentor, Jerry!

If the mentorship is of longer duration, you can include milestone reviews at 3, 6, 12 and 18 months or whatever works for the length of time.

Ending the mentorship

Given the temporary nature of mentor relationships, the time to end them will inevitably come. Your program should include a procedure for doing this effectively.

In many cases, especially in association or corporation mentoring programs, there is a finite time period and this is important. But if the relationship isn't working, just as when you're dating, or in a bad partnership, it's important to know when to let it go. Here is some guidance on when, and what to do for both scenarios.

Let's start with a situation where there is a mentorship platform—I've included a sample below, with permission, from one of the programs that I was engaged in. Having how-to's is useful, as navigating technology can often be challenging.

Generally, these are the steps to follow when a mentee hasn't been responsive, and I've seen this happen in some of the industry mentorship programs I've been involved in. The person disappears after follow up, or the mentee wishes to end it.

How to end a mentoring relationship in a platform [sample from Mentorly]

Note: A timeline should have been established upfront, so that the ending of a relationship is not a surprise.

- Log in
- Click on Relationships
- Click on the mentor or mentee you would like to end the relationship with
- On the right hand side, click "End Relationship"
- Should the mentoring relationship not be a good match, have a conversation with the other prior to ending the relationship.
- Tips for the conversation:
    - Restate the original goals and objectives about what you were hoping for out of the relationship
    - State that they've helped you achieve all those goals
    - Thank them for their time
    - Let them know you will be taking care of this in the platform so they won't be surprised when receiving an email.
- However, if a significant period of time has passed (ie: 10 or more months) without any contact, you may wish to

just end the relationship through the system. This can be done in person or in writing via email if there isn't a platform to formally do it.

You have now had an opportunity to review some of the roles or styles of mentors, what responsibilities and capabilities are key and tips on providing guidance to the mentor in your program. Now let's move over to the roles and styles of mentees and how they can make the program successful as well.

6

———

ROLES AND RESPONSIBILITIES OF A MENTEE

"Every great achiever is inspired by a great mentor.

"Every individual must be given the opportunity to unearth their highest potential." —*Lailah Gifty Akita*

Now that we've reviewed the various roles of mentors and how they might work in a relationship, let's consider the other side of the relationship. It's important to outline the roles and responsibilities of the mentee to help you build these into your mentorship program. Keep in mind that a lot of this applies to a traditional top-down mentorship program, yet there is value that can be applied to any type of mentor relationships, outside an organization as well as_within. Here_are a few ideas on_how to support the mentees in your company, and an overview of the styles and roles that mentees may embody.

Mentee as Student

One of the first times a mentoring relationship may form is earlier in life, often between a teacher and a student. As a student, the mentee is always learning something. Think back to all the teachers you've had, and how some of the best ones mentored you.

This can apply to all the categories of mentoring discussed so far. The mentee is always learning something, and is in essence the primary student. In a reciprocal mentorship, each participant is a student in some way. Many of the mentors I spoke with in my research said they also grow and learn from and with their mentee.

The mentee might look for a mentor who will teach them something new. They want to develop a new skill for their career, or how to be more confident, or a variety of other topics. It's generally up to the mentee to find the right mentor, one who matches their learning style as well as aligned expertise in the new skill they want to learn. If your organization has an initiative, the mentor program manager can help find the right matches. Or if you are a large enough company to use a mentor platform, then profiles will be in the software and a mentee can find someone they resonate with.

The mentee as student will absorb the mentor's knowledge and has the ambition and desire to know what to do with this shared knowledge. They may practice and demonstrate what is learned in order to achieve their agreed-upon goal. The mentee decides upon the amount of help and guidance they need, and takes the initiative to ask for help or advice and to tackle more challenging assignments.

As I mentioned earlier, having some resources or advice when I was an articling student in a mentor relationship might have made a huge impact on my start in the legal profession.

The role of mentee as student is one of the most common approaches to mentorship in the workplace.

Mentee as Apprentice

An apprentice is similar to a student in that learning is involved; however, an apprentice receives more hands-on guidance and training.

A mentee may want specific guidance rather than general advice. Formal apprentice training programs often include mentoring. One example is the program at Keystone Development Partnership[1], where it is viewed that mentoring is best accomplished as part of a formal apprenticeship training program with certain conditions.

First, classroom training provides students with basic theory and general understanding. Then hands-on instruction applies that understanding in the classroom, in a lab, or in a controlled work environment.

Finally, the apprentice works alongside an experienced professional on the shop floor so that they can apply the new knowledge and skills to their real jobs, which they will be expected to do every day. "On–the-job training is intended to be mentoring in its purest form," says Chuck Hodell in his book *ISD From the Ground Up* where he talks about ground-up training and on-the-job mentoring training.[2]

The apprenticeship aspect of the relationship is a time-limited, structured process conducted in the mentee's own work area to help them perform specific tasks. The mentoring aspect, on the other hand, is ongoing and provides more general guidance on gaining pertinent job skills.

The mentee as apprentice is more aligned to training as opposed to–general development. The mentee is receiving information and demonstrations and then assessed. The 2017 guide created by Keystone Development Partnership is an excellent resource to review this approach.[3]

Mentee as Protégé

Over the years I have mentored a number of women, and also been in reciprocal mentoring relationships, mainly with early career women. I always used the terms *mentee* and *protégé* interchangeably. But could there be a difference? I did some digging to find out.

As it turns out, the various dictionaries identify these two words as the same, so linguistically the terms are synonymous, and which you use is really just a matter of personal preference. Here are some of the dictionary definitions for your reference.

Mentee
Collins dictionary:
someone who is mentored
Miriam Webster:
one who is being mentored; protégé

As discussed earlier when we looked at sponsorship, often a protégé is a person who receives significant support and promotion from someone more established in a field. A protégé is typically given special favours or status.

Often the word is used for someone who has exceptional or standout talent and is taken up as an upcoming star or powerhouse. The word's original associations, however, have nothing to do with talent and everything to do with how a person treats the protégé—the source of the word refers to protection.

Let's review in more detail, because there can be differences.

The word "mentee" is a derivative of "mentor" and implies_that the human mentee is simply an extension of their mentor. Some people view mentees as those who are really in need of help, and often the volunteer mentor programs look at their mentoring for young people who may be at risk, or in trouble, and so that's why they need a mentor. That's not always the case, but it's historically how these relationships developed.

The word "protégé" is not derived from "mentor". The relationship is mutual. Think of a protégé as a star or gifted person who is destined to follow in the footsteps of greatness, and then to excel beyond the work or success of the mentor. The mentor often seeks out the protégé, so I see these types of relationships more as sponsorship.

In some cases the mentee needs help changing from their past, and in some cases the mentee has a gift that the mentor identifies and sees as part of the mentee's future. In my view this should be the case with all of the relationships. Yet you can see that the mentee as protégé takes the mentoring to a whole new level.

Mentee as Intern

Historically, an internship was a pre-requirement to obtaining some type of designation or license. An intern is often hired and trained in a well-documented process, with quantitative terms and measured by strict standards. For example, in the architectural industry, it is a structured and mandatory process that must be followed in order to become a certified architect. It is similar to my articling experience to become a lawyer.

In this way it is similar to the apprentice, and often intern and apprentice are used interchangeably. In both cases, the learner must meet these skills or they don't obtain the designation.

Today, however, many people bring interns into entry-level roles, and some in fact have been taken advantage of with low pay or sometimes no pay! This has now been addressed in Ontario with a law passed forbidding free interns unless they meet certain exceptions.[4] This will be a rant for another day!

To summarize, a student, apprentice, protégé or intern are often the roles that mentees may adopt in organizational mentor programs.

I've reviewed the roles a mentee might play, but there are also some functions in the relationship that are recommended for the mentee to take on. Here is a rundown of those functions.

Driver of Relationship

In traditional mentoring, the mentee is in charge and the driver of the process. It's critical that the mentee understands that the mentor is here to support, not monitor, and that their time needs to be respected. Here are a few things the mentee can do to be in the driver's seat:

- Identify the skills, knowledge, and/or goals they'd like to achieve and communicate them to the mentor.
- Bring up new topics that are important at any point and give feedback to the mentor.

- Create the experience by defining boundaries, timelines and structure.

In your mentorship program, you can provide the resources to guide mentees to do this.

Development Planner

Like any good project manager or planner, the mentee needs to be creative and put together the plan, ideally with resources and documentation developed by you as the employer or program manager. For example, the mentee might:

- develop and maintain a mentoring action plan (or agreement)
- work with their mentor to set up goals, developmental activities, and time frames
- schedule appointments and keep them
- set agendas for each meeting

Sometimes some of these are available documents within a system/platform, or other times there is a form that can be completed to assist with some of these aspects. If not, the mentee might develop it.

Resource Partner

Once the mentee has decided on goals and objectives, they can ask their mentor to provide some specific guidance. The clearer the mentee is in leading the process, the more success they'll have. Here are a few ideas on what a mentee can do to get the resources required. They can ask their mentor to:

- provide or help find resources for specific learning
- recommend books for growth and development

- identify other people that might be helpful and ask for an introduction
- identify milestones or sub-goals with the mentor's help

Ideally, if the company has a checklist all these different processes will be a lot easier to accomplish. See the Life Works Well website resource section for samples.

Teacher

I've mentioned my personal bias towards reciprocal mentorship, as I think today that is where the enriched learning comes from and the deep connections can be made. You'll learn later about Lisa Fain and her organization Center for Mentorship Excellence, and her passion and belief that all mentoring is reciprocal. In her view all mentorship relationships must have reciprocity. I believe this is true in most cases, but there remain traditional forms of one-way learning and giving.

For the relationship to be successful, the mentee is also often teaching the mentor. The function of teacher may not always be relevant (especially in traditional mentorship), yet the mentee can do the following:

- Look for opportunities to give back to the mentor
- Share any information that might be valuable based on discussions
- Recommend a book that was impactful
- Identify skills the mentor may want to develop
- Teach the mentor some skills they have, like social media, technology or AI

Continuous Learner

The primary role of mentor relationships is to learn and grow, and this is one of the main reasons people mentor or are mentored. The mentee may:

- Take full advantage of this opportunity to learn
- Provide a clear objective of the area of education required
- Review the learning and once developed, choose something else to learn

The mentee will generally want to continue their growth journey and this is a key role that they might adopt.

Responsibilities of Mentee

Now that we've looked at some of the various roles of mentees and the functions they perform, let's look a little closer at the responsibilities. Some say that mentees are too inexperienced to have responsibilities. I disagree.

The mentee will grow and learn a lot more if they actively take on responsibilities and lead the way!

To be involved in a mentoring relationship is a privilege for both participants, and it is important that both parties are gracious and considerate towards each other. If you're part of a mentor program, and you are unclear about what to do or how to act, please seek guidance from the program manager if there is one, the mentoring resources available, or ask your mentor. If it's an unstructured mentorship, ask your mentor or a friend/colleague. Trust, respect and open dialogue is ideally already established.

What are some of the qualities that an ideal mentee might possess when they participate in your mentor program?

Here are some ideas, and you can create your own expanded list that aligns with your workplace or organizational culture.

- Eagerness to learn
- Ability and willingness to work as a team player
- Patience and empathy

- Openness to be a risk taker
- Embracing a positive attitude
- Commitment to appointments
- Accountability in all aspects

To create the responsibilities list you need to develop some recommendations or guidelines and some ideas for you are set out below.

Be Respectful of Time and People

Although the mentee is generally the driver of the relationship, initially the mentor might take the lead. So, the mentee's responsibility is to listen and respect the opportunities, limitations and format of the relationship that the mentor can provide. Respect and courtesy are a top priority responsibility, and without this no trust will be built and likely no success in the mentorship.

During discussions with the mentor, the mentee can also use active listening skills. Don't interrupt. If you do need to clarify a point, wait for a pause or opportunity, or write a note to follow up so you don't forget. Take notes when appropriate, ask good questions and have a purpose for questions. Silence can be awkward, so going back to the role of planner makes sure each meeting has an agenda. The organization hopefully has developed resources to help with this.

Set Goals and Objectives

Going back to the roles that a mentee plays, at the outset of the relationship the goals and objectives for the overall relationship need to be developed; this could be about the career or sometimes even personal goals. Within each of those goals you'll need to carefully manage each meeting with the mentor so you're on track towards those goals; this is no different than what you might be doing with your manager at work, but it's to do with the goals of the mentorship, not necessarily your work objectives. The mentee should be prepared to ask for specific guidance and advice on goals, plans and strategic ideas. The more specific the goal, the easier it will be for the mentor to help.

There are many platforms that track this. Take for example, MentorCity, which was used by the Human Resources Professional Association (HRPA) for a decade, and the platform we used when I was Chair of Chapter Mentorship. I'm a member of this organization and was actively involved in their mentorship program. This platform has developed over the years, but there are many platforms available if your mentor program will be large enough. When working with this organization, even 30 or 40 people who are participating in a mentor program can benefit from tracking in a system. If there is budget and the company is large enough these technology tools help; if not then a simple spreadsheet or fillable form helps with account-ability.

Assessment and Feedforward

The term feedback often has a negative connotation, and some orga-nizations are replacing feedback with feedforward, the term coined by Marshall Goldsmith, which I love. While feedback by definition focuses on the past, feedforward aims to give information that will help in the future.[5]

The mentee is the one who can take the initiative to ask for input on how things are going. Feedforward makes it less difficult, as it comes across less as criticism or negativity. The organization might create a structured process for this input and dialogue throughout the program, as it is vital to a mentee's personal and professional development. The mentee needs to demonstrate an openness to hear new ideas and suggestions.

Remember the earlier discussion about identification of strengths and Stand Out 2.0 (Marcus Buckingham)? This is a wonderful way to change your feedback model to a more positive one!

We discuss how you might also measure the program later in the book. Allowing the participants to provide their input, qualitatively and quantitatively, will help you enhance your program and ensure its success.

The mentee can ask for guidance and input on specific issues, such as written communication skills or presentation delivery. When a mentee asks for specific details this also needs to address and understand specific behaviours. In addition to asking for this input, the mentee might also identify how they receive best. For example, does the mentee like direct or softened messages, or is humour an effective method?

As I've said before, it's all about building trust between the participants, so in the process of building your program ensure you have tips, checklists and resources available to help mentors and mentees at the outset of the program. This will help bring about a worthwhile return on investment.

One cautionary note before we move to the next responsibility. Whenever there is dialogue or communication between mentor and mentee, neither participant should go on the defensive. It's human nature to do so, but it does not help. The key is to level set at the beginning, and determine these expectations upfront. The mentee can ask for this type of conversation from the beginning so that when it's time for the mentor to provide some honest and open feedforward, it's received well. The mentee should thank the mentor for taking the risk to be honest and, *vice versa*, the mentor should also be open to this from the mentee.

If you've read Brené Brown's work, then you know that being vulnerable isn't always easy, but it strengthens connections and bonds between people, and this applies to mentorship as well. Remember, if the mentor was not invested in the relationship, they likely would not have taken a risk to be open. Honest input gives an opportunity to grow and enhance skills, and will inevitably help the mentee move towards fulfilling the goals and full potential.

Time Management

The mentee is always considerate and respectful of the mentor's time (and yes this also applies to the mentor). Time management applies to the overall tenure of the relationship (i.e. is it six months or one year?) as well as the length of meetings, texts, phone conversations or other methods of taking up time. The mentee needs to be thorough but succinct in explanations, experiences and comments. Being aware of cues and watching for clues takes practice. No one wants to be called the rambler or known as the one who has never-ending run-on sentences. That's why having an agenda for meetings is important and the mentee won't have to worry about talking too much or not being efficient and productive in meetings. It is polite to ask directly about this.

Much of what I'm talking about here applies to all types of relationships both personal and professional, but since the mentorship is likely something that is not the mentor's full time work it is important to truly respect time. The mentee ought to remember to return phone calls promptly and be on time with commitments or meetings. If the mentor offers a specific time frame of availability, respect this by following through. Keep in mind important family or other commitments, but that's where setting up meetings in advance and getting the timelines and calendar set up helps. Only extend the time period allotted if the mentor initiates or insists to extend or complete a task or discussion. While life does get in the way, it's all about the commitment you want to make to moving towards those goals.

Implementation

The mentee needs to seriously consider all advice or suggestions received. While functional conflict is encouraged, arguing why the mentor's advice would not work can be construed as rude and closed-minded. The mentor is there because they have a lot of experience and generally have been in similar situations. Politely discussing reasons why the advice or guidance might not work, and backing it up with real data, will increase respect between you. It's all in the delivery. Don't be afraid to voice your opinion as a mentee, but deliver it with respect.

If advice is given and there are actionable steps that the mentee can address, this needs to be executed on. It's a waste of everyone's time and it is disrespectful to be in a mentorship if the mentee isn't going to commit to change and growth. Like any other project at work, ideas might come easily, but it's all in the implementation!

The mentee can demonstrate that the advice was followed and that commitments for action at every opportunity have been identi-fied_and implemented, even if it means a modified plan. It's agile mentorship like any other agile work project. Being able to point out that the mentor's help was addressed and sharing outcomes is impor-tant, both in the relationship and in the metrics if the program is being measured. This strengthens the trust and connection between the two participants.

On the flip side, the mentee may not agree 100% of the time with the advice and guidance of a mentor. Sometimes there may be values misalignment or the fit isn't right and they're feeling uncomfortable. This is a time to reconsider and perhaps end the relationship. Becoming more confident as a mentee and aware of your own deci-sion-making processes is something that can be built up as part of mentoring.

If the goals were clear at the beginning, then generally the advice given is related to that and there shouldn't be any issues.

Ideally, when the mentorship has run its course, the mentee is ready to become the mentor and the ripple effect starts.

Express Gratitude

While not a typical responsibility, expressing gratitude and showing appreciation for every form of assistance a mentee receives is recom-mended. This can also be applied to so many different situations in the workplace. Studies have shown that gratitude has a positive impact. A meta-analysis referred to in the Chronicle of Evidence-based Mentoring says the research offers clear guidelines for incorporating gratitude into mentoring programs.

Write a thank you note or email at various milestones in the process; and while emails are lovely, take time for a handwritten card for something special. A mentee should make only positive or neutral comments about the mentor to others, unless they are giving feedback to a program manager. If you disagree with the mentor's values, behaviours, or attitudes, discuss it with the mentor directly. This is a two-way relationship so the idea of mentor with heart applies, as does mentee with heart. Respect the mentor's confidence and trust. If the mentee isn't aligned with the mentor and their values, it might be time to look at ending the relationship, and that is discussed more below.

It is scientifically proven that gratitude can help change a brain's neuropathways. Even though many mentors are giving their time and knowledge freely, a little thank you can brighten their day.

Confidentiality

Assume the mentoring connection will be strictly professional and confidential. This is generally established at the outset. This does not mean that the mentee should not be authentic or can't be friendly or funny. It simply means it is up to the mentor to take the lead in establishing a more friendship-based connection. Many people have talked about how the mentorship started out professionally and continued for years, where eventually they became friends, or chosen family.

Neither mentee nor mentor should intrude into the other's personal life or expect to be close friends. Any romantic involvement is obviously inappropriate. Ensure the mentoring connection does not give the appearance of favouritism or inappropriate romantic aspects. Often the mentee might share personal details, and the mentor also needs to respect the boundaries of the relationship.

Therefore, it's critical to have the guidance available for both parties. Sharing personal information does help grow a connection and relationship so long as the confidences are kept private. This will help build the trust that is the most important ingredient of any mentor relationships. MentorCity has a document for establishing safety in the relationship.

Attributes and Responsibilities for Mentees

Remember that true mentors are heart-centred and truly believe in the value of mentoring. Similarly, there are a few specific characteristics that a mentee may also strive for.

The mentee is inspired to be:

- committed to expanding their capabilities and focused on achieving professional results
- clear about their personal and career goals, needs and wants. Mentees create the mentoring agenda based on the results they hope to achieve, so they must be clear on what those are
- willing to ask for help, be vulnerable, and explore different paths
- receptive to trying new ideas. Mentoring doesn't work if the mentee isn't open to learning!
- able to seek and accept all feedback or feedforward, even when it's painful—and act on it
- personally responsible and accountable. Mentors want to see movement and growth. Do what you said you would do, when you said you would do it.
- willing and able to meet regularly on schedule for the long term

Tips for mentee starting with a new mentor

It will be helpful to your participants if you provide some guidelines for starting the process of a new mentoring relationship. The following are some ideas for the mentee to consider at the beginning of a mentor relationship.

- Establish a protocol for contact and response times and what is acceptable.
- Determine whether they will hold meetings in person or virtually, as well as where, how often, etc.
- Decide what can be shared and what must be kept confidential.
- Determine mentoring boundaries, what is up for discussion and what is not.
- Ask the mentor what their expectations are of the process of giving and receiving feedback.
- Share goals and ask mentor how they will each be held accountable by the other.
- The process will be much more successful if each party makes the effort to get to know the other personally. This can take time, but it's the best way to build the necessary trust.
- Each party needs to be clear in their mind why they are doing this, and what they expect to get out of it. A successful agenda for the relationship will depend on this clarity early on.
- At regular points in the process, they should each check in with the other to evaluate how each sees progress to date. Necessary "course corrections" can be made based on this feedback.
- When they reach a predetermined end date, parties should reflect on their experience, identifying the most rewarding and valuable aspects of the relationship. At this time they should express appreciation of each other, including specifics about what they took away from the experience.

Being organized will go a long way to making the mentorship relationship successful.

Tips for mentee to end the mentorship

What happens if the mentor has gone into hiding, or the meetings are awful? It might be time to end the mentorship relationship. A lot of time and effort is put into making this work, especially in organizations if done well, but if it's not working let it go! It's kind of like dating—after a while you just have to leave the relationship.

It is important to be prepared to move beyond the mentoring connection once it has served its purpose. It may simply be that the relationship has run its course and it's time to move in a different direction.

I don't recommend that you ghost your mentor, as you never want to burn bridges. Here are some tips on how a mentee can end it respectfully and lessen the pain!

- Be sure to end on a positive note.
- Keep the door open to return to the mentor for assistance or advice at a future time.
- Follow up with the mentor after the mentorship ends to keep in touch and to share progress.
- Continue to express gratitude.
- If it was a non-match, respectfully do the above and provide feedforward as to why it's ending in mid-stream.
- If the goals have been met, then explain that and figure out a plan for what's next.

For more detailed resources like this, check out the Life Works Well website. Now that we've looked at the various roles and responsibilities of the mentee, let's move on to some guidance on implementing a mentor program in your organization.

7

———

IMPLEMENTING A MENTOR PROGRAM

"If you are intentionally looking at mentoring, that is probably an indicator that you are thinking about employee engagement, career development, and retention and attraction in top performers." — *Cindy Bush, CHRO*

It takes careful planning to create the right mentor program for your organization, and one size does *not* fit all.

People responsible for implementing programs may assume that they can replicate the same program at every organization they have worked in, but this is not usually the case. While there are some basics you can apply to all programs, there are a number of other significant considerations before implementing a mentor, coaching or sponsorship program.

While the focus of this book is mentoring, this chapter outlines a methodology that is often used in any type of project or program management initiative. I've taken my decades of experience with world class organizations and adopted the best standards that have worked in the past. While these guidelines are often customized, they've proven to create amazing results and successful outcomes for the companies and clients I've worked with.

Program Implementation Methodology

As you've no doubt guessed by now, I am very much in favour of developing a mentorship program for your company. The sad fact is that many corporate mentorship programs fail. That's because it seems so simple that we think, "Mentoring—how hard can it be?", and then, of course, it turns out not to be simple at all and we make some mistakes along the way.

I don't want that to happen to your program, and that's why this chapter is a "how to" overview to help you do it right the first time.

At a high level, here are the phases I normally recommend for any type of program implementation, including an application to create a mentor program.

1. Know your "why" first
2. Do your research
3. Determine the type of program
4. Finalize your business case
5. Identify your implementation team
6. Get final executive team buy-in
7. Create resources and guidelines
8. Identify reviewers/participants, partners/decision-makers
9. Educate all impacted groups
10. Determine measures/metrics and time period
11. Communicate and engage with your employees/participants
12. Review, revise and renew

Let's review each of these phases as applied to implementing a mentor program.

Phase 1: Know your "why" first

Like your business mission and vision, you have to think about why you want a mentor program. Are your competitors getting the best and brightest talent because they offer one? Are there any retention and/or promotion challenges within the ranks? Will mentoring help address employment equity requirements or diversity, inclusion and belonging opportunities?

Knowing your "why" is going to be the most important thing you understand before embarking on this process. Once you've landed on this, then you can start to develop your program and project plan. It may not warrant a full-blown charter as used in major technology or large-scale projects, but applying sound project management principles and structure to any corporate program is excellent practice. This also should include aspects of the business case, which will be discussed more fully in Chapter 8, once your research is completed.

I recommend applying this disciplined approach to all major program and policy implementations, as it forms a methodology and process structure to use, and details won't be forgotten. Depending on the size of your business, you may also want to create a change management and communication plan. In fact, I highly recommend this as part of the work packages.

Make sure your leadership is on board from the beginning. Rather than have one-off informal mentoring or a grassroots approach, have the most critical or impactful information and an executive sponsor who will support starting the initial research. You need at least one advocate at the senior level who will help set the stage and champion the initiative. A well thought out plan will help convince leaders to go for it.

It may be relatively easy to get HR, Talent Management and employees on board, but if you don't have strong support from leadership, you won't get the budget, the resources or the ability to attract strong mentors for your program. You won't get to the next phases without executive support! So have enough data to support it, and then dig in deeper to the rest of the research below once you get the go-ahead.

In the last several years, mentorship has grown and I understand that there isn't as much push-back, so go for it—if not now when?

Phase 2: Research—External and Internal

Further in-depth research is the next phase. Keep in mind that all the processes shared here can be completed on a step-by-step basis and phased approach, with some overlap. This is particularly important if you're a small business and the sole program manager or HR generalist wearing many hats. For medium to larger organizations who have access to more resources and people, your research, internal and external, can be completed at the same time as your initial review or other phases. For a mentor program you won't have many legal factors to consider, but that is part of project management for many HR initiatives.

Generally, some research is completed at the beginning as you're trying to figure out what type of mentor program to create. Do you want a mentor circle, group mentoring or one-on-one traditional program? Research helps narrow this down and aligns with your "why". Perhaps you have more than one type of mentor program in mind.

What are your competitors doing? You may want to offer something unique and ideally better than the others so that you stand out. If you've determined through research that a mentoring program is required, let's get it done! Leadership will expect results, so get it started.

Internal research includes discovering what your existing employees want. Have your survey or pulse checks identified the desire for development? Have you asked about interest in mentoring, coaching or other support? Are there some examples of grassroots or organic mentorship where participants want to spread it more formally? Metrics are key, so you need to identify any data you have as part of your research to drive the business case. You also need to identify potential gaps between your current state and ideal future state.

External research can also include studies mentioned in this book and examples of companies that have had success with mentor programs. All of this information might be part of the project research.

I have been part of organizations that had what I called "underground" programs, where the mentoring opportunities were not communicated very well or only provided to the "chosen few". In other cases, there were siloed approaches, where some areas of the organization had outstanding programs and others lacked the opportunity. While there is a need to create the right type of program, remember that your employees talk, and they will find out if some people are getting preferential treatment. Yes, you want to reward top performers, but many others would get there if they had mentors, and these inconsistencies can start to breed negativity and disengagement in your workplace.

Your external research and internal research can include:

- Academic published studies
- Other resources such as mentorship books
- Papers, blogs and articles on the internet
- Top employer award summaries
- Other company case studies
- Competitor landscape summary
- Internal and external benchmarking/metrics
- Internal data from surveys and focus groups
- Internal demographics of potential participants
- Participants identified and executive buy-in achieved
    - e.g. review committee and project teams
    - Whether to include a technology platform

When I began working in the field of mentorship about 72% of Fortune 500 companies had programs. In 2024, 98% of Fortune 500 companies offered some type of mentorship program.

There is a myriad of information available to help you—topics such as how to find a mentor, how to be a great mentor, company and career mentor programs, and more. Google searches show millions of results, so that's why I have included some of that information throughout the book and on my website. With the adoption of artificial intelligence, such as Perplexity.ai or ChatGPT use caution when obtaining sources and validate them. I have navigated and condensed best practice recommendations from a number of these resources all in one place, and included my unique perspectives as well.

Reflect demographics of your organization

Another thing to keep in mind is that your program should reflect the various generations and demographics within your organization. Let's review the generations for a moment.

For the first time in history, there are five generations in the workplace, so there is plenty of information exchange and wisdom to be shared among all generations. The five generations currently are:

- Traditionalists: 2% (1925-1945)
- Baby Boomers: 25% (1946-1964)
- Generation X: 33% (1965-1980)
- Generation Y (Millennial): 35% (1981-2000)
- Generation Z: 5% (2001-2020)[1]

I believe the majority of the traditionalists have long ago left organizations and now play more strategic roles like advisors, board members or consultants. Or they may be finally enjoying their well-deserved retirement years.

The Baby Boomer generation, born between 1946 and 1964, are now retiring, and 65% of them expect to work until at least 65. They are ideal in traditional mentor roles, their company knowledge transfer is important and this wisdom can be passed on to Gen Z who are entering the workplace.

The Millennial (Gen Y) generation grew up with technology. They are the ones who helped executives in the reverse mentoring programs I discussed earlier. Gen Z grew up with devices, so communication styles are different, instant messaging is a norm and mentoring them will be different. You need to think about how to gear your mentor programs to those demographics.

It is likely the Gen Xers will help out with traditional mentoring, and perhaps those Baby Boomers who are not financially able to retire, or simply want to keep their brains in a growth mindset.

Technology Platform Needed?

Another part of the research is determining whether you will use mentor matching software. I think it is important to research the technology available depending on the size of your organization. Manual matching through use of Excel spreadsheets is not sustainable in the era of data analytics, and can only work for a small company with few resources and a smaller number of mentor pairs. The investment is likely worth exploring for most companies.

As a side note, with the pace of change in technology there are frequent updates. When I started research for this book there were a dozen or so mentor platforms I was familiar with. At the time I worked for a payroll and HR services and technology company and was always on the lookout for what was new in the HR tech industry. Now there are about 20 to 40 well-known mentor platforms and this is growing rapidly (maybe 100 now), so you need to check out what is right for your organization.

If you decide you will require a mentor platform that links to your learning and development technology platform, you'll have to include that as part of your research and implementation plan, and at least have a sense of these costs when presenting your business case to the executive team for approval. They will not want any surprises. Many of the platforms will give you a demo, and also provide costs (usually based on per user models).

Other areas to consider for your research include:

- Identification of types of mentorship programs
  - Traditional program?
  - Reciprocal and peer-to-peer?
  - Group or circle?
- Tools and Resources
  - Mentor agreements, goal documents
  - Software platforms available
  - How-to's, guides and tipsheets
- Measurement criteria
- Structure of program
  - a more formal relationship with commitment or organic/informal

Phase 3: Determine type of mentorship program

For this phase you should revisit the research from internal data and analysis to decide what type of program you want. As with other programs, your internal surveys, focus groups and needs analysis will drive the why and the how.

Do you want a buddy program at the start of onboarding, mentoring for the first six months for new employees? Or do you want something more structured like ongoing mentor programs for new leaders, for equity initiatives or group mentoring with a particular set of skills development? We covered a lot of this in other sections of the book.

We reviewed the various types of mentor programs in early chapters and this is where you need to decide and identify the types of mentor programs. Is it only one? Is it several? Is it a traditional program or reciprocal, peer-to-peer program? Is it mentoring groups or circles? You should have an idea of the type of program you want.

Now is also the time to address thoughts on structure, resources and support you will have or create, and handling of any challenges or issues. Like any relationship, where many things can happen, if you haven't talked about how you will handle issues ahead of time, a mentoring program can get sidelined if you haven't thought through big decisions.

It is always a good idea to have two or three options to present and the challenges and benefits of each. It is also a good idea to recommend a pilot program to test first.

If you need help with this, you can consider hiring a consultant who has created these programs. How will you select and pair mentors with mentees and mentees? How will you train mentors and protégés? How will you evaluate the program? A qualified consultant will save you time and money in putting together a well-thought-out plan.

Phase 4: Finalize business case

Creating a business case is a skill that not everyone has developed. It doesn't need to be overly complex for a mentor program, but you will wow your executives if you have taken the time to create an executive summary, why this program is a must-have, the costs of implementation outlined (time, resources and financial costs). If technology is required for larger companies as mentioned above, you will want to touch on the return on investment for this as well.

If you are a human resources professional who is implementing a mentor program, highlighting your financial acumen and business side is going to help your career as well.

The business case components will vary depending on how many types of mentor programs. Is it only one? Are there several? Are you using software? and more. The business case template is a guideline, and you can pick and choose whether all components are necessary. For example, if you are a larger company, you may also want to use a mentor platform software and that adds complexity and cost to your business case.

We review this in more detail in the next chapter, but at a high level this is what might be included:

- Executive summary

- Project definition
- Business requirements
- Evaluation of options
- Preferred option
- Strategic logic of project
- Benefits
- Risks
- Project/program stages and duration
- Financial analysis
- Estimate of project team resources
- Decision makers
- Project authorization
- Appendices

The complexity and robustness of your business case will depend on the size of the company, number of employees, how many programs, and more. The business case will be much simpler if it is a pilot for one small area or group, but going through the exercise will help guide you. The next chapter will walk you through this.

Phase 5: Identify implementation team

The key to success is ensuring that the right person is going to run the mentor program and the right team is assembled from initiation phase to review and implementation. Ensure the program manager is an employee who will have accountability for it (for example, they might be from the Learning and Development, Talent Management or the Policy/Program team). Most of all, the program manager should be committed to the idea, have a passion for mentorship and want to lead it. It's also essential that the program manager has the support of the executive sponsor.

Other team members may include a business analyst, technology expert, learning and development expert, communications advisor, and a legal representative if necessary. You might engage focus groups and others if possible, and identify ahead who is going to develop and review the tools and resources created, as well as the documentation for training and communication materials. There is a lot that goes into this, so don't leave out any details.

You will be identifying the potential participants: who is impacted, such as managers; other collaborators needed to make it a success; and who the final decision-makers are. This is covered in Phase 8 (or simultaneously here).

Your mentoring program might not be successful if it is assigned to an employee who doesn't believe in it, or by assigning its creation and implementation to an employee who is not invested in the idea, who has too much on their plate already, and who will not be evaluated for their work. The creation, implementation and management of a mentoring program requires someone skilled in strategic thinking, communication, organization, as well as the ability to network effectively with employees at all levels.

That's why it is all about creating a culture where mentorship is also an everyday event, there are mentor moments throughout, and that everyone mentors with heart. The right mentors will also make a huge difference in your workplace and in any mentor relationship.

Phase 6: Get executive final buy-in

Before you start investing all of your time and energy in creation of the documentation, development of training, resources and communication plans, check in with the leadership team to make sure the project still has a green light. Priorities frequently shift, and you don't want to start on work that will be shelved.

This has happened to me. I worked for several months revising an existing program that I didn't develop originally. I sought feedback, was updating materials, adding new Q&As after a new program had been launched and there were several unanswered questions that weren't anticipated.

These processes are all part of ongoing program management to enhance it going forward. We were just about ready to launch the revised program when it fell victim to cost-cutting as the organization was going in a different direction and the economy was not faring well. It happens! Luckily in this case the new program initiative we designed saved the organization millions of dollars in the long run and some of the work was not completely lost.

Get that final buy-in! Then get to work creating the supports, tools and resources to make it a success.

Make sure you've planned frequent milestone updates for decision-makers, and get green lights throughout the process.

Phase 7: Create resources and guidelines

A common mistake in creating any type of program, whether a mentoring one or not, is that tools and guidelines or checklists are simply created and updated to a website or internal portal without effective communication, education and frequent updates. If it's a new program, it's a little easier than something that existed with more complex change management requirements, but additional guidance is sometimes required.

If you want the program to have impactful results, you need more than documents for people to read. Provide mentors and mentees with education like any other type of training, such as in person workshops or guided videos. Maybe you can be creative and launch the program with videos from senior leaders who will be mentoring, or the CEO if possible. Get people excited about it! These videos can also be part of the possible resources.

Often people think that mentoring is simply a matter of pairing mentors and mentees, and they will be fine on their own. This is far from the truth. As I discussed in detail in earlier chapters, the right pairing, like the right wine with the right food, is important. Like any relationship, there needs to be agreement and communication. For example, how often they will meet, what is confidential and what isn't, and what role the mentee's manager might have.

Include all of the guidelines and tips in ideally digestible bites, and just-in-time learning as required. Make it a memorable "fine dining" experience.

Phase 8: Identify Participants, Reviewers, Partners and Decision-Makers

While this is also important at the outset, others impacted beyond the implementation team are important to consider. Who will be the mentors/mentees, what area of the organization is going to pilot the program?

Who should be reviewing the draft resources, guidelines, documentation as part of the program development? When does the marketing/communication team get involved. As mentioned above, some of these phases are often happening at the same time. The purpose here is to continually review who is impacted by the program so that there aren't any surprises.

While we used to call these people "stakeholders" and continue to do so, the world is changing and this language that had colonial roots is being reconsidered, I prefer "impacted groups".

The more excitement and buzz you create, the more engagement and success you'll see.

Phase 9: Education of Participants

Educating the participants in the mentor program, and reviewing the resources as part of the learning and development, will get the partnership off to the right start and set it and the overall program up for success.

Some of the tools or resources that might be used in addition to technology software are:

- Guides for mentor/mentee
- Tip sheets
- Recommended books
- Icebreakers and discussion topics
- Feedback guidance
- Measurement dashboards
- Mentorship agreement, goal setting documentation

You'll find some samples and ideas for some of these topics if you head over to the Life Works Well resources section.[2]

Ongoing communication and check-ins are also beneficial. One great example of this is HRPA West Chapter's mentor program. In the beginning, some of the other chapters were getting more traction than the West. After implementing more frequent communication and ongoing check-ins and surveys of the participants, the chapter went on to surpass its goals from 2020 onward. One of the interesting things that the outgoing Chair of Mentorship, Angie Vincenzo implemented was the first vision board workshop for mentors and mentees. This was a fun way to engage members and encourage participants to get involved in the mentorship program, and create their career and personal goals together in a creative way.

I became the Mentorship Chair for several years after Angie, and continued this annual tradition, although most of it was virtual during the pandemic period. With a wonderful committee while I was Chair, we were able to grow the West chapter mentor participation by 50%. Our Chapter Chair, Michael Greenwood, was extremely supportive of building on the mentor program and we had remarkable and noticeable results. Michael said that these results were due to the commitment to communicating regularly with our members, providing virtual and hands-on training and education and creating fun and engaging events for mentors and mentees to connect. This was one of the highlights of my career and enhanced my already existing passion for mentorship!

One of my mentees, Sania Sanzgiri, and I were also featured by the HRPA, highlighting our long-standing mentor partnership in their mentor program! Sania also co-facilitated a few events with me, and later became a mentor to others embodying the ripple effect in action. You can add some fun and excitement to your mentor programs through creative networking events.

Phase 10: Determine measures/metrics and time period

Once you've decided what type of program you are implementing, you'll need to touch on the measurements and metrics.

Again, a reminder to determine the organizational needs and reasons for the mentor program you choose to implement. You will want to create metrics that will measure those organizational goals (increase retention, improve employee engagement, track promotions, performance, etc.).

Ideally the organization already has solid data analytics on a number of the metrics below. If not, a baseline is required so that some measurement of the program can be ascertained.

- What are current retention rates?
- What are "Glassdoor or other reviews/stats" about the company?
- What is found in historical internal survey results?
- What are promotion rates at various levels?
- How many employees already participate in organic mentoring?
- What are some qualitative measures employee satisfaction?

Is a mentor platform or software required to help with metrics?

As mentioned above, one major decision you will need to make is whether or not to use software as part of your program. For large organizations this may be cost efficient as you are matching hundreds or even thousands of pairs, but for smaller businesses it may be cost-prohibitive. There are some tools that can help with this part of the analysis, as well as with measurement/metrics. For example, Together, has a handy calculator and return on investment guide and MentorCity has a business case template and other resources. You can find more on their websites and review.[3]

Here are some thoughts on using software and some of the goals:

- Helps manage / make the connections and matches participants
- Tracks enrollment (number of participants)
- Tracks activities, such as number of hours, meetings, reaching goal milestones
- Summarizes analytics and reporting

Here is a brief list and examples of available software, mentoring platforms:

- MentorCity
- 10KC (Ten Thousand Coffees)
- Together
- Mentorly
- Chronus
- Insala
- Mentorloop
- Mentorcliq

These are only a few of the possibilities. Please keep in mind that I am not advocating for any one of these organizations. I have experience using some of them, and can advocate for those companies, and I have spoken to many who have used other platforms.

When I first started researching and working in the field of mentorship in 2017 there were about a dozen or so platforms that I was aware of. At the time I was working for a payroll/HR technology company, my passion started to grow, and I was often exploring tech companies who had mentor programs. Today at the time of the publication of this book there are well over a hundred mentor software platforms to choose from, and thousands of companies mentioning mentorship as part of their offerings.

If you decide to use software, choosing it will take up a lot of time, it will require a request for services analysis and process, involvement from your technology experts and the right team to assess the best platform for your organization.

Phase 11: Communication and Employee Engagement

I recommend making the roll-out of your new mentor program offer something exciting. Try to make it as much fun as launching a new product out to market. Have your CEO do a welcome to the program video or have a launch party with speed mentoring or mentoring icebreakers as part of it. You want to inspire as many employees to participate as possible, both as mentors and mentees. Later on, you can have mentors and mentees champion the program and share their success stories.

Communication and training are key, and your mentor program should be part of your existing learning and development strategy. Make sure that there is a communication plan, who needs to know what, what is key messaging, how is mentorship celebrated, hold speed mentoring and networking events to get people involved. Be creative and have fun!

Here are some ideas for every stage of your program launch.

Pre-Program Communication

- Clarify the program's purpose and desired outcomes for both mentors and mentees.
- Share tangible benefits for mentors (leadership experience, recognition) and mentees (skill development, networking).
- Get buy-in from senior leadership (endorsements via videos, email blasts, memos, town halls).
- Circulate the mentorship proposal to department heads or team leads, emphasizing alignment with organizational goals.
- Launch a visually compelling recruitment campaign (desk-drops, posters, intranet announcements) to attract mentorship participants.

- Be transparent about selection criteria (time availability, areas of expertise or interest).

Mentor–Mentee Matching Communication

- Use application or intake forms with structured questions (career goals, interests, communication style, availability).
- Provide a clear timeline and selection criteria for matching.
- Organize a short, orientation-style kickoff (in-person or virtual) to outline program expectations and introduce participants.
- Send individualized match emails summarizing relevant strengths, interests, and goals for each mentor–mentee pair.
- Or if technology software is being used provide training and outline on this.

Ongoing Program Communication

- Schedule regular check-ins (monthly or bi-monthly) to monitor progress and identify challenges.
- Conduct mid-program surveys to gather feedback and adjust as needed.
- Provide mentorship toolkits (conversation starters, goal-setting templates) to guide sessions.
- Offer communication templates to help participants request updates, share achievements, or discuss difficulties.
- Maintain an open forum for mentors and mentees to reach the program coordinator with concerns, feedforward and suggestions.
- Offer conflict-resolution guidelines (outlining next steps if a pairing isn't working well).

- At the halfway mark, have a webinar with a guest speaker to motivate participants.

Post-Program Communication

- Host a wrap-up event to share success stories, recognize achievements, and gather final feedback.
- Distribute completion certificates or badges to celebrate participants.
- Use an anonymous feedback form to evaluate program effectiveness and gather suggestions for improvement.
- Consider a three-to-six-month follow-up survey to measure any ongoing mentor–mentee engagement and program impact.
- Create an alumni network or group to maintain connections and exchange mentoring best practices.
- Encourage former mentees to become future mentors, ensuring program sustainability and growth, and starting that ripple effect.

General Communication Tips

- Use clear, inclusive, and encouraging language in all messaging.
- Maintain consistency in communication rhythm (weekly updates, monthly newsletters) so participants stay informed.
- Use multiple channels (email, intranet, Slack/Teams) for easy access to information.
- Promote transparency and open dialogue about goals, expectations, and scheduling constraints.
- Incorporate storytelling or testimonials to highlight mentorship success and inspire ongoing participation.

For other resource samples please head over to the Life Works Well website.

Phase 12: Review, revise and renew

It is important to evaluate the program at various milestones and this should be part of the planning. Establish timing of these reviews and assessments as part of planning. For example, six-months, one year, annual each year after.

Leaders will support continuing a mentorship program when you demonstrate a return on investment (ROI). Your business case should have set out the potential ROI, but it's important to validate this with them. The studies at some organizations mentioned earlier measured over several years, and you'll also want to measure qualitative and quantitative feedback in the first year. Your mentoring program will sustain itself when you determine, ahead of time, the business reasons for creating the program and how you will evaluate success.

In my experience of creating and implementing successful, long-lasting people and mentoring programs and being a part of many others, when you follow a structured program development and implementation process, your mentoring (or other) program will gain traction and be more successful. I truly believe that mentor cultures will lift up everyone in the organization so that they can be high performers and happy employees. It is one part of a heart-centred culture, and your company culture and bottom line will be the envy of all your competitors. I've seen many companies win awards for their mentoring programs.

So, what are you waiting for? Go propose your mentoring program now.

The next chapter focuses on the Business Case in more detail. This may or may not be required in your company, but it's also a useful outline for any program or project you may want to implement.

8

THE BUSINESS CASE

"You must strengthen the case for mentorship by showing how it contributes to critical company goals and talent outcomes—things like keeping talented employees, helping them grow and building essential skills. Showing these connections with solid data helps everyone understand the real value of mentorship."—*David Wilkin*

You're an HR or business leader who hopes to implement a mentoring initiative within your company, and you want to ensure you have all the return on investment (ROI) numbers, data and research organized. This part of the book takes the early stage of program development I outlined earlier on research and business cases and breaks it down to save you the time and effort.

I summarize some of the research and case studies and provide a number of ways for you to crunch your data. This step-by-step business case development is one of the most important parts of your work, as it will help you measure the ROI and success of your mentor programs and apply it to your company. Here we go.

You have finally completed the research and have an executive sponsor. If you're lucky you may not need to create a formal business case, but going through the exercise will help you prove or measure the success of your program if asked. This phase helps you create a business case to take to the next levels of approval.

How do you do this? I have some ideas to share with you.

Whether your company is a scaling business and you want a simple onboarding mentor program, or a mid-to-large-sized company and want a full-on mentor program with various offers, what I set out below can help you get organized. If you work for a non-profit or trade association and want to offer a mentor program to members, the ideas here will help you piece together a solid business case to wow the leadership decision-makers or board members who need to approve it.

While implementing a mentor program may not be as complicated as creating a new product to sell or investment required such as a complex accounting system, the business case document includes a number of key components. The business case is particularly critical if you want to include mentor matching software.

Based on my years of experience developing and implementing programs and products at CIBC and ADP Canada, as well as for many clients, I guide you on what a business case document might cover. In addition to internal training while at CIBC for project and change management, I learned from Chase Consulting Group out of Australia[1] and with permission I adapted some of their key features into my unique methodology. If you want to dig further into their 5 Step Business Case training[2] or other resources, you can review their offers.

Components of a business case

For any initiative, program or project you wish to implement, there are a number of things to identify in the business case, as outlined below:

- Identify key objectives and business need
- Provide context of the investment, including important background and supporting information

- Identify alignment of the investment with the organization's strategy
- Estimate the costs of the investment, and its financial and non-financial benefits
- Describe the planned timelines, resources, procurement and governance
- Assess the inherent risks, their possible effect on the investment and the strategies for mitigating them
- Be clear about the level of uncertainty around the program
- Provide the management and/or the board with options to consider in reaching their decision

I cover each of these areas for a mentor program in detail below. I am going to use as an example a fictional company whose leadership team wants to explore a mentor program. Let's call the company "Healthy Life". They offer health coaching and sell nutritional products online and in brick-and-mortar locations, so there are a variety of functional departments. The company has 1,500 full-time employees and 750 contractors and/or seasonal workers at various locations.

As there are always competing priorities within any organization, a well-prepared business case will help your project be recognized and successful. Your goal is to have your program approved, so it's imperative to help the executives see its value.

The business case template is listed below (and you can pick and choose whether all components are necessary). For example, if you are a larger company, you may also want to use mentor platform software, and that adds complexity and cost to your business case. Some companies will use technology even if there are only 50 employees in the company, so you could go ahead and ask for approval for it. What have you got to lose?

Here are the technical headings of the business case (and some of them from the Chase Consulting method), although you may not use all of them:

- Executive summary
- Project definition
- Business requirements
- Evaluation of options
- Preferred option
- Strategic logic of project
- Benefits
- Risks
- Project stages and duration
- Financial analysis
- Estimate of project team resources
- Project authorization
- Appendices

Let's look at these components individually. Remember for your mentor program(s) it may not need to be complicated, and will depend on scope, size of company, number of participants, whether you use technology, etc. You can also find a sample template on the resources page of Life Works Well.[3]

Executive Summary

This section covers the overview of the program and its key objectives and generally is one or two pages at most.

Describe which mentor program you want to build. Is it a traditional one? Peer-to-peer? Onboarding buddies? Or a combination of several? For the Healthy Life example, we are recommending a structured mentor program, with three options to choose from.

This summary needs to be crisp and clear and capture the attention of the decision-makers. Insert and highlight some of the statistics I've provided throughout the book. For example, in 2020 the Vistage CEO Confidence Index indicated that 86% of CEOs surveyed agreed that mentors were a crucial part of their career accomplishments, and 98% of Fortune 500 companies now have mentorship programs.[4]

Create an impactful and direct Executive Summary that highlights the key decision points, the why behind the initiative, the costs and the outcomes to be measured.

Project Definition

Here is a sample of how to define your project for a mentoring program, applied to the fictional organization Healthy Life for the sake of the business case.

Healthy Life embraces a culture of holistic health, and our core values are health, kindness and growth. With this in mind the mentoring program will help participants and our organization in the following ways:

- Identify and achieve goals for career development and personal growth that also support business objectives
- Create a culture that embraces our values and mission by helping others
- Support leadership development in embedding our core values
- Foster higher levels of engagement and career vision and advancement
- Develop the leadership skills of empathy, kindness and other abilities
- Give participants tools and resources to help them become healthy, high performers and heart-centred leaders and employees
- Position Healthy Life as the sought-after nutritional and holistic wellness company to attract top talent and in turn more customers.

Business Requirements

The business requirements will be based on your needs and size of organization. For example, if you are a large corporation that will make the mentor programs available broadly, you may also be considering the technology aspects in addition to the tools and resources.

Business requirements generally include thoughts on end-to-end project implementation and utilization and measurement of the program.

A list of types of business requirements might include the following:

- Resources to design, implement, communicate and monitor program
- Financial resources (for people if new, and/or technology implementation)
- Duration and length of commitment of program(s)
- Verification of participation of mentors/mentees
- Determination of type of mentor program
- Metrics and return on investment analysis

For the Healthy Life example, you would want to address that the employees are spread out over many locations, so virtual mentoring will be required and you may need to cost out technology. You may also want to identify a pilot group of employees first; for example, one specific department or an onboarding mentor program for new employees.

Evaluation of Options

When you propose a few options rather than one type of mentor program, your business case needs to evaluate them. For example, maybe you want to propose more than one type of mentor program. Or perhaps you believe that various types of mentoring programs are suitable. In addition to traditional top-down mentoring you may wish to implement an onboarding mentor program, virtual speed mentoring sessions, peer-to-peer or mentor circles or reverse mentoring.

It's always a good idea to have up to three options for leaders to consider so that at least one of them is approved! This is the time to be creative, yet thorough, and present viable options.

As mentioned, I recommend that you pilot the initiative first (for larger organizations), but it's a balance since you want to be inclusive and not have some groups of employees feel left out.

One of the goals is to ensure that everyone has an opportunity to be mentored or to be a mentor at some point in their career journey.

Taking the Healthy Life example of implementing a mentorship program, here are the three options I would set out at a high level:

Option 1: Traditional mentorship (top-down approach)—all employees who wish to participate have access to a one-on-one mentor

The mentors should volunteer and be measured. Creating a mentor culture means that everyone buys in and commits. The best way to do that is to have it as part of performance goals and measurement.

For our example of a 2000+ employee company, you may need technology in the future and put out a request for services. However, you may wish to pilot with a certain group of employees and will use Excel spreadsheets or Google Sheets for matching mentors/mentees.

Applying this to the Healthy Life example, recommend a traditional program be rolled out with testing one department as the pilot, for example all product sales staff. Pair leaders or experienced team members with those with less than three years' experience so that you are measuring the success over a 12-18 month period. You can have a combination of sales leaders in corporate and in the store location matching with newer sales team members; you'll have to address in-person and virtual options, but this gives a good testing group.

Option 2: Mentor Circles or Peer-to-Peer Group Mentoring

The identified mentors will facilitate mentoring for groups if one-on-one is not feasible. In this case, the mentors who volunteer will be provided with education and support to ensure an excellent experience. Participants will be provided with a curricula-based experience based on similar needs, skills development and career level within the organization.

Guidelines for this program will need to be established, and I recommend you set this out as well. For example, specifics on what skills will be developed. Is it sales, leadership, confidence-building, or other identified upskilling needs in the company? Give the decision-makers this detail.

For the Healthy Life example, identify the mentors and potential group members to start. In this fictitious example suggest the mentors be C-suite leaders who will mentor next level senior executives. Each C-suite executive has a domain expertise they can share, such as sales, finance, customer service, etc. and the model for group mentoring can be passed down level to level in the organization, embedding it into learning and development. This will also give you buy-in from the top!

This is how you can start a ripple effect of mentorship in your organization.

Option 3: Onboarding Mentors

Every new hire will be provided with a mentor for the first six months of work, to help onboard and to develop an understanding of the ins and outs of the organization.

The mentors assigned will meet with their mentee once per week for the first month, every two weeks for the next two months and then once per month for the next three months unless they'd like to meet more frequently.

Applying this to Healthy Life, this is another easy way to pilot mentoring. The needs are a bit different as onboarding mentoring is really more about introduction to the company instead of formal skills development. This option could be for the virtual new hires or all new hires and a consistent format created, and is time specific so can be measured quickly.

Preferred Option

As the lead on the project, you should have a preferred option with recommendations on why you want to implement that option, with return on investment (ROI) metric proposals to support it. Remember, you need your current data so that you can measure and compare and address the needs (i.e. retention, job satisfaction, skills building, etc.).

Using the above example, Option 2 is the one I would recommend because it will reach the broadest number of people and engage both existing team members and new hires at Healthy Life. With success here, you can then roll out to other areas. Option 3 is only for new hires, so it limits the number of people who will benefit. Option 1 is too much at once, and contingent on having enough mentor volunteers.

Since change management is always a part of implementing new programs, you may want to start smaller, test out the program and then expand once it is measured.

Another reason Option 2 is a preferred option is that you can have those who would like to participate facilitate groups of people with the mentor circles or peer-to-peer group mentoring with cross-functional options and not hierarchical. You will have to accompany your choice with the data, costs and expected ROI.

Strategic Logic of Project

This section may not be necessary unless it is a more sophisticated, lengthy project (for example one that also includes implementing and training on the use of mentor platform technology). This is divided into four components and your business case should cover each one at a high level:

- The Problem or Opportunity
    - underlying problem or opportunity (your 'why' for mentoring)

- Outcomes and Benefits
  - more detail on how the mentoring program benefits the organization
- Strategic Response
  - the various initiatives/options, for example how retention and development is being addressed through mentorship
- Business Inputs
  - how the program will impact the ROI

A lot of these ideas were set out in earlier chapters of the book.

Benefits of the initiative

I have addressed the benefits of mentoring throughout this book, but for the business case you know your leaders and decision-makers like statistics, so this is where you can shine. Again, depending on what type of program you are implementing, you will want to pull out the right statistics and research on benefits, and below I provide some possible sources to review and include. You will have to identify your current retention, promotion and attraction numbers and how the program might enhance them.

Individual Benefits to Mentees

When identifying the benefits to mentees in your business case to decision-makers, you can cite some of the below (pick and choose what makes sense for your culture and workplace). From my review of the multitude of studies and research[5], reported outcomes for mentees include:

- Job security
- Higher salaries
- Higher-level positions in organizations
- Enhanced political and social skills

- More work satisfaction and lower job turnover
- Better understanding of roles, responsibilities and job satisfaction
- Confidence and happiness, improved perspective
- Enhanced well-being

This equates to higher retention, lower costs for talent acquisition, and increased positive employer brand. You will need to understand your metrics on retention to begin with so that you can measure the ROI of the program after a mentor program is implemented. For example, after six months or one year in the pilot group has there been longer retention? More promotions? Apparently, some new hires have been leaving quickly if they don't like the culture, so if you've kept them one to two years and beyond and it is linked to mentorship, it is a success.

Remember that this is a long-term plan, so you may not see results until a couple of years after the program begins (for retention, attraction, promotion, etc.)

One substantive analysis reviewed over 40 mentoring research studies and found compensation and promotion to be higher in mentored individuals (in comparison to their unmentored peers); higher career satisfaction; greater confidence in the advancement of their careers; higher job satisfaction; and greater intention to stay.[6]

If you are the type who likes to do your own research, there is also an excellent collection of articles and other resources found in a summary on the state of mentoring, coaching and other developmental networks for those who would like a more academic review.[7]

Individual benefits for mentors

In my research, the interviews I conducted and feedback as a mentoring consultant, I confirmed that mentors gained as much as the mentees in a program.

This is supported by studies that show the following benefits for mentors:

- Raised professional identity, visibility and career revitalization
- Enhanced leadership skills
- Self-satisfaction and improved perspective
- Greater confidence and happiness
- Improved psychological health[8]

In the Sun study mentioned earlier and below, mentors were promoted six times more often (Sun, 2009). These initial studies are often mentioned as we are only recently seeing more case studies from the mentor platform organizations, and it will be important to update any further data on this in your own research.[9]

Benefits to the organization

The combined benefits to mentors and mentees also translate into organizational positive outcomes. Benefits at the organizational level include a more satisfied workforce, commitment, motivation and retention of employees, higher morale, higher quality work relationships and better leadership.[10]

In an earlier study by Hegstad & Wentling[11], the five most frequently cited impacts of the formal mentoring programs were:

- retention (59%)
- promotion and advancement (35%)
- satisfaction (35%)
- morale (29%)
- productivity and performance (29%)

We need more up-to-date information for companies in the future. For more details, you can explore the sources from Knowledge at Wharton, Art of Mentoring, and Evidence-Based Mentoring, companies that provide research and discuss the broader impacts and methodologies related to mentoring programs.[12]

As noted earlier, Gartner and Capital Analytics conducted a study on Sun Microsystems' mentoring program. The study examined more than 1,000 employees over a five-year period and found substantially higher retention rates for participants in the mentoring program compared to those not in it. This is where an often-quoted 72% higher retention rates for mentees originally came from. The retention rates for mentors were 69% at the time while the rest of the organization's retention rates was 49%.[13]

At the time, Sun Microsystems reported savings of $6.7 million in avoided turnover and replacement costs, and the ROI was over 1000% from their mentoring initiatives. The study also found that 25% of employees in a test group who took part in the company's mentoring program had a salary grade change, compared with 5% of employees in a control group who did not participate in the program. Mentors were promoted six times more often than those not in the program; mentees were promoted five times more often than those not in the program.[14]

There is a substantial amount of published information on the impact of mentoring on productivity. One organization, TNT, asked mentees to estimate the productivity improvement they had achieved as a result of mentoring and 48% of survey respondents said they believed they had more than a 50% improvement in productivity.[15]

Another organizational benefit that is often overlooked is the leadership capacity development of mentors who participate in a mentoring program, which offers them both training to enhance their developmental conversation skills and an opportunity to practice those skills with someone who does not report directly to them.

Since the earlier studies there was not a lot of published data on the benefits of mentoring, but over the past decade the mentor platform market has grown and with it more data to support the benefits of implementing mentor programs in an organization.

In the Healthy Life example, put all of this information in a summarized form or appendix, especially highlighting the benefits to the organization. The benefits section could be used for any type of mentor program you implement. You will want to link the data to your own company, your Why; in this case connection helps employees with their well-being and this is a key outcome of mentorship, important for a health company! It is likely you would provide a few of the key metrics and statistics and then put the rest of your research in an Appendix for those who want the facts to back up the recommendation.

Risks

In this section of the business case, you identify the risks of the program/initiative. Risks can include financial, legal, reputational, time etc.

For example, if there is a cost associated with implementing the program (and there always is—see section on costs) a risk may be that implementation costs are much more than you thought. For example, maybe the technology cost, if implemented, was higher than anticipated.

You may also experience an impact on your employer brand if word gets out that it's a poorly managed mentor program and you've been using it to entice new talent. Or if the naysayers won't buy in due to internal politics, there is a risk of impact to your engagement scores and company reputation.

The key here is identifying the risks and having a mitigation strategy to address or avoid them.

For our Healthy Lifestyle example, if you're proposing options there may be some slightly different risks with each, so state the general ones first, then anything for a particular option. With Option 2, the risk may be that there is turnover for the mentors leading the program, or the mentors aren't trained/educated on how to mentor groups well and this could impact qualitative engagement results of the program. Or you could identify that virtual mentoring may not be as effective to build connection. The key is going through this process so you're prepared for the questions.

Project/Program Stages and Duration

This was covered in detail in the last chapter on end-to-end program implementation. Depending on the size of your project (for example if you have thousands of employees and will use mentor software, etc.) then you may want to assign a project manager and manage that way. If it is a smaller company or a pilot, then a Program Manager or the HR Lead can generally act as the project manager as well. Be careful as it's important to pull together a team that has various responsibilities rather than one person wearing all the hats.

Set the project stages out clearly for the leadership team, including check-ins for milestones, and the length of the program, etc. I recommend a weekly check-in to ensure the project is moving forward on schedule.

One key component is communication—the better the communication the more successful the program! Do not forget this as this is often overlooked.

And I always recommend a post-implementation debrief for lessons learned and how to enhance the program in future. With the right approach and commitment, you will be successful.

We won't cover examples for Healthy Life as this is identified in detail in the previous chapter. You've got this!

Financial Analysis

I've had to learn to love the money side of program implementation —understanding the finances didn't always come easily to me. I credit my improvement in managing budgets and analysis of costs to one of my leaders in HR at CIBC who taught me a lot about the finance side, and I adopted this to running my small business. If you want to be successful, your leadership team and the decision-makers will want to know the numbers, any cost savings (retention dollars saved, etc.) so spend time on this part of the analysis.

Throughout the book and the ROI section, I've set out some samples of metrics you can use, but you need to apply that to your organization. If you don't have the baseline numbers then you need to get those in place first (e.g. retention or turnover stats, promotions, engagement score, cost of replacement, qualitative and quantitative analysis is needed).

For our Healthy Life example, the company will want to look at the retention numbers for the groups impacted for each option; what are the sales staff retention and turnover numbers? How many sales people get promoted? What is cost of replacement? The same for all companies link to your existing measures and then at the end of the pilot mentor program did things improve? If you're hiring someone to manage the program then that is cost to include.

Estimate of Project Team Resources

Identify the team members, and how much of their time they will spend on this project. For example, is it a weekly one-hour meeting along with two to three hours of research or tool development? Is it for six months, one year or longer? Be realistic about setting up the expectations, but if you advise your leaders that you have a great starting point by following the methodology set out and having the research at your finger-tips you will likely be more convincing.

Time is money, as you know, so make sure there is a huge reward to the organization, and minimal wasted resources. In the Healthy Life example, you'll want to identify how to address anyone in remote locations if they are part of the initial project team, and for the team developing the program, the anticipated time involved. Link productivity and job satisfaction to your ROI. If your team is already stretched and taking this is on top of an already hectic pace, it may impact success. Keep people healthy and happy!

Project Authorization

Document who makes decisions, who reviews project milestones, who will authorize the go-ahead for the project. Get the approval signed off in writing and any budget set aside and pre-approved. This will avoid any unexpected hurdles when you are ready to implement.

Appendices

The Appendices for your business case should include the various resources or draft templates/tools you may have already developed. Remember the business case and executive summary should be a high-level overview and speak to the approvers (and ahead of time, when possible, to ensure buy-in). The appendices are back-up to show you've done your homework, and you can reference some of the many statistics and data provided here.

One of the most rewarding parts of a career is implementing a program or initiative that made a difference in the lives of others. That's what mentorship is all about, and I wish you huge success!

There are a number of resources throughout this book and on the Life Works Well website to get you started and thinking about your business case and bringing mentorship to your organization. And you can reach out anytime to ask questions.

Start that ripple effect of giving and growing!

9

HOW TO FIND A MENTOR OUTSIDE YOUR ORGANIZATION

"Know what you are looking for before you seek a mentor. Do your research and align your values to the relationship and industry you'd like to be in."—*Liz Shorten*

Your organization may not have a mentor program, or you may not feel comfortable with a mentor inside your company for a variety of reasons. Maybe you were passed over for a promotion too many times. Perhaps you are ready for a new role, a bold change, or don't align with the company culture or values. Or you may be looking for a completely different career path, or want to start your own business and feel you need a confidante from outside the company or a new industry.

This chapter is designed to help you find a mentor that works for you.

You will notice that this chapter is a little different from the rest of the book. In the course of my research, I interviewed about sixty people with extensive leadership, career and mentoring experiences, and here I address a number of aspects of finding a mentor by blending their comments with my own experience and ideas.

In some cases, where the person's comments were extensive, I have paraphrased them. In other cases, I simply quote a sentence that further enhances the topic of discussion.

I hope you find some inspiration from these everyday mentors as we explore how you can find the right mentor for you outside your current organization.

As we have already covered, meaningful mentorship will provide the guidance, knowledge, and skills you need to grow in your career and personal life.

How do you choose the mentor who will help get you where you want to be in your career or life? How do you decide who is the right match? How do you know the relationship will be successful?

Let's take a look at some of the ways you can find your meant-to-be mentor outside your company.

Understand Why You Seek a Mentor—Know What You're Looking For

Before you begin your search for a mentor, you must understand why you are looking for a mentor and what you aim to achieve from the relationship. You need to be thoughtful and intentional before you start approaching potential mentors. Having studied the concept of *Ikigai* and applying it as a coaching method, starting with your why or purpose can be applied to mentorship as well. For more on this concept check out the resources below. [1]

As Joanne Trotta, Leadership Development Coach and Facilitator, suggests, you must get really clear on what you want. Do you want to learn new skills or gain some additional knowledge? You need to have clarity on the desired outcomes of the experience. If you as a mentee need help but you don't know what you need help with, it won't be an effective mentorship.

Virginia Brailey, CEO, Growth Strategist and Executive Marketing Leader, reiterates this, and adds that you don't have to have it totally figured out, but you should have some idea going in if the relationship is to be successful. Virginia also confirmed my belief that commitment is one of the most critical components for it to be successful, and "what you put in you get out." Virginia is actively involved with the American Marketing Association (AMA) mentor program and has mentored countless professionals inside and outside the organizations she worked with. She also mentored many women while at ADP Canada and helped me at work when I was going through a very difficult time in my personal life. Her everyday mentorship was exactly what I needed.

If you want to find a mentor relationship that will be meaningful and long-lasting, first take the time to do some deep thinking about what you want to focus on.

One key step to knowing the "why" is to identify your goals. Do you want to develop new skills? Do you want to gain knowledge? Do you want to switch careers or start a business? Do you know what areas you want to grow or develop in? Answering these questions will bring clarity on where you need guidance and will help you decide what you are looking for in a mentor.

You must also take full responsibility for your actions and choices. If you want to find a mentor you need to own the process and not expect to have things land in your lap.

Janice Stillo, former TD Bank Leader, suggests that mentees have to make the effort and find the solution as well as identify what they are looking to get out of the mentorship. You have to find those answers—it's not up to the mentor. She also says you don't necessarily need to have a long-term objective right away. You can have simple objectives and small milestones as a starting point. Janice has been a long-time friend and mentor, and we also did some work together when she was leading a group mentoring program at TD Bank. Holding space for the mentee to decide what their area of focus will be is also critical at the beginning of the relationship.

This is confirmed by Hendrik Steenkamp, Sr. Program Management and HR Transformation Leader, whom I also worked with while at ADP Canada. According to Hendrik, as a potential mentee you need to be open to identifying opportunities to grow and develop. You need to be very honest with yourself and determine what you are missing in your life, career, and what you need to get better at.

Tim Cork, President and Founder of Straight A's Inc., Author, Coach and Leadership Expert, says you also have to approach a mentor thoughtfully. He recommends going to that person with your successes, your challenges, and how they can help you with these. He also suggests knowing your top 5-10 goals.

Tim believes it is okay for you to push back and challenge your mentor from time to time, and never be complacent or totally comfortable.

> "You go from your 'what', to your 'why', to your 'how' and 'who'."— *Tim Cork*

Now that you are clear about your "why" and reasons for wanting a mentor, let's look at your mindset and some ways to ask.

Develop Courage, Network and Simply Ask

According to Tracey Poulin, HR leader, some people are afraid to ask for what they need, either because they feel vulnerable or are worried they'll lose their credibility for what they already know or worked really hard to know.

If you don't already know the person you would like to ask to be your mentor, networking is a great way to meet and connect with potential mentors. Connect with many people to determine who will be the right fit for you. Meeting others outside your organization allows you to compare your compatibility with other new mentors. Growing your network might also help you find mentors for other areas in your life.

Building confidence takes time, so the more you put yourself out there the easier it gets. And caution, don't start pinging every influencer or thought leader saying "Hey will you be my mentor?" While I suggest you be bold, sometimes it will rub people the wrong way if that's the first thing you ask. It's okay to approach someone you admire, but go about it in a thoughtful fashion.

You can do what June Tavenor, CEO of Catalyst Health Solutions, and Registered Nurse, suggests and "date up"! "When you think someone is out of your league as a potential mentor, forget that—reach out, absolutely reach out." I agree with June that you should go for it, but I'd add that you must be prepared and know your "why" before you approach someone for mentorship. Building relationships and trust takes time.

June also advises not to be afraid to end the relationship. If you're in a relationship, either as mentor or mentee, that's not serving you any more, then let it go. We covered this earlier in the book and this applies to any mentor relationship whether inside or outside your organization.

The theme of being fearless applies in so many aspects of our lives. While it might seem intimidating to approach someone you don't know, there are ways to take your time and ease in. For example, you can start following them on LinkedIn, Instagram or TikTok, commenting on posts, and seeing who else in your network might be able to make an introduction down the road.

If you're in HR you probably know about Hacking HR and the Founder, Enrique Rubio, who created this movement during the pandemic to connect HR people all over the world. His first piece of advice is to look for a mentor and his second piece is, "Don't be afraid of what's going to happen." He encourages you to go ahead and seek out that mentor who has gone through the journey that you think you'd like to embark on. There is somebody who can show you a better way.

"Number one, seek out mentors. Number two, be fearless!"
—*Enrique Rubio*

Since I first started writing, Hacking HR has now added mentorship to its community offers. Find the community or association where you might find your next mentor; there are many out there.

Remember, those who have gone before you may have made mistakes so they can also guide you on what not to do. Some of the advice might resonate and some might not, but the main message here from me and many I interviewed, is do not let fear get in the way!

All of this is reiterated by Sarah Wells, Speaker, Coach and Olympian, whom you met earlier in this book. She says we are often afraid because we don't know everything and we are worried about looking silly. Sarah advises you to be brave enough to ask for help. Be comfortable with the fact that you may feel silly because that person might be someone you admire or might be further along in life than you are, but that's why they are a great person and resource to ask for help!

I couldn't agree more—that's the first step. I wish I had been brave enough to ask for help when I was younger. I thought I could do it all on my own and that I didn't have anyone to turn to. Now that I'm wiser, I continue to seek out mentors and coaches today, and continue to grow, and get out of my comfort zone by going for it.

Before I close out the idea of networks and finding people to support you, I want to share another thought that I discussed with Heather Haslam. Heather was the last manager I had when I worked at ADP Canada and a huge support to me when I was making a decision about my future career. I would have loved to continue to work with her had it not been for my mom's declining health and my own exhaustion at the time. Heather and I spoke about the concept of a Personal Board of Directors when I interviewed her. In addition to successful and not so successful mentor experiences, Heather relies on those close to her and in her network to provide different perspectives. She nurtures these relationships, from an ex-boss to a mentor to her brother, they will call her out on her "BS" and be there when she needs them. Not everyone can be everything to you so having a group of people you can go to is another way to expand your growth and learning.

Your future mentor is waiting for you and may be right in front of you!

Where to look for a mentor

Where do you begin to look for a mentor outside your company?

I mentioned LinkedIn and other social media platforms as an excellent way to connect with others. Now that the world has opened up after the COVID-19 pandemic, you can start attending events. Look for an industry association or community you can join, preferably ones like the HRPA or AMA that have mentor programs and start to get yourself out there.

Stacey Dakin, Chief Program Officer, President and Chair of Lean In Canada, says if you're looking for career mentorship, then you need to take time to build your network. You need to attend events either in person or virtually. You need to read people, follow people on LinkedIn, follow them on Twitter, read their posts so you can engage with them, comment on their stuff, then send them a message.

Stacey shared with me her experience after a tough job loss. She was busier in the weeks after losing her job than she had ever been in her life, because of the people in her network who reached out to her. She reached out to many and several contacts agreed to have a coffee break with her and spend forty-five minutes talking about what she wanted to do. This was extremely beneficial. She says this happened because she had many unique mentors.

Through her prior work with Mentor Canada, Stacey also helped shape the future of mentorship for Canadian youth. This type of organization can also help mentees find a mentor, especially youth in high school, college/university or early career.

I talked a lot with Stacey about having a mentor mindset, which essentially means you can mentor frequently, what I like to call being an Everyday Mentor™. It doesn't always have to be for a lengthy period of time—you can have one-off mentor moments. For example, if you're an entrepreneur there are organizations like Start Up Canada, and Start Up for Women who can help you find a mentor for even one conversation. I have met so many incredible women starting businesses who have reached out to me this way as a mentor through the programs with Start Up for Women. This is why I also created the initiative *One Million Mentor Moments (OMMMs)* to encourage mentorship beyond formal programs.

Tracey Bissett, Professor, Centennial College, CEO Bissett Financial Fitness is an excellent mentor for students and those in the early career stage seeking to get comfortable with finances. She is also the brains and voice behind The Young Money Podcast, and Tracey's advice is to meet many different people, don't be too quick to ask them to be your mentor, and a person doesn't need to mentor you indefinitely. You can be mentored in one conversation, much like the idea of mentor moments and being an everyday mentor. Tracey has also mentored many women entrepreneurs providing much-needed guidance on the financial aspects of running a small business.

> "You can get mentorship in many different places and you can be mentored in one conversation."—*Tracey Bissett*

Networking is key, but many people struggle to figure out *how* to network—well that might be a topic for another book! You can find tons of resources and mini-courses on how to network well. I'd also add that "netgiving" is part of building up these connections, asking what can I also give to others? This is a term I first heard from Tim Cork that sticks with me today. More on that in the future!

This is a learned skill that isn't easy for everyone. Be creative in how you approach people. Tim Baker, HR Leader and Consultant, confirms the need for informal networking. Tim used to co-host DisruptHR Toronto and those events have started up again so that is an excellent way to get out there and meet people especially in the people and culture field. He recommends building up your network, finding someone there you can connect with or align with after you get to know them a little bit better. Perhaps they can do some informal mentoring with you. Tim also reiterates the advice that you must know what you are going to ask before you approach the potential mentor.

Tim suggests checking out the platform Ten Thousand Coffees

(10KC), to which I'll introduce you later. The platform works as a micro-mentoring space as well as traditional mentor and sponsor matching platform. When you reach out to people make sure to let them know what mutual value there is.

The message seems clear! Start connecting and networking with others. You've got this!

The People Already in Your Life

You may already have mentors in your life—what I referred to earlier in the book as organic mentoring. Look at those people already in your network, not only the influencers or leaders on LinkedIn (even though they are valuable too). There may be someone you have already built rapport with who is willing to continue the relationship on a more formal mentoring basis.

Stacey Dakin says it's important to have more than one mentor. According to Stacey, you have to look for a variety of mentors and you need to recognize that the people closest to you are the ones that make the best mentors because you have access to them. There are people already in your life that you have developed trust and understanding with, and it's a matter of asking if they are open to more formally solidifying the mentorship. And of course, one-off mentor moments and mentor mindset is available at any time.

> "It could be a friend's brother, it could be your grandmother, it could be a neighbour. You know, those are the easy, everyday mentors."
> —*Stacey Dakin*

Zahra Shaikh, Sr. Product Marketing, found one of her first organic mentors at an early stage of her career. She found this relationship more naturally and her mentor was focused on giving back. They had the chemistry, she felt comfortable asking him to mentor her and this continued after he left her organization.

"Some people in your life are already your mentors—you don't necessarily need to make it official."—*Zahra Shaikh*

Find an Industry-Specific Organization with Mentor Programs

The most efficient way to find the right mentor that matches your needs is to look for mentors that are experienced in what you want to improve on. And also make sure you are comfortable with them, and this is likely given they have walked the path before you. For example, if you are a new immigrant to Canada, you might want a mentor to help you navigate the Canadian work environment or offer guidance on how to progress in your professional career. Companies like Toronto Region Immigrant Employment Council (TRIEC), YMCA, Mosaic and Windmill can help.

Here are five top mentor organizations that provide support to new immigrants in Canada:

YMCA Mentoring Program for Immigrants

This program focuses on helping immigrants integrate into the Canadian job market by offering a four-week mentoring program. It includes sessions on job search strategies, resume building, and interview preparation. The mentors are experienced professionals who provide practical guidance and networking opportunities.[2]

Culture Connections Social Mentoring Program by MOSAIC

Based in British Columbia, MOSAIC's program pairs newcomers with volunteer mentors who help them adapt to Canadian life. The program includes weekly meetings, access to local events, and networking opportunities. Mentors, often immigrants themselves, assist newcomers with language skills, cultural adaptation, and social integration.[3]

Windmill Mentorship Program

This program is part of Windmill Microlending and is designed for skilled immigrants. It pairs mentees with professionals in their field for six months, providing guidance on career options, networking, and skill development. The program is especially beneficial for those looking to advance their professional careers in Canada.[4]

Toronto Region Immigrant Employment Council (TRIEC) Mentoring Partnership

TRIEC's mentoring program connects skilled immigrants with mentors in their field. The program focuses on helping mentees understand the Canadian job market and workplace culture. It has a strong network of corporate partners and is known for effectively supporting newcomers in securing employment in their professions.[5]

I spoke with Janine Travers, Learning and Development Leader at CIBC, and she has been involved in the program there partnering with TRIEC to bring a multitude of diverse employees into their organization through the mentor programs. Janine also shared about one of her first mentors who happened to be one of her managers. She had so much respect for him and he had a huge desire to share his wisdom and knowledge. Throughout my discussions it was clear that connection and comfort were key with mentor relationships and in Janine's words, "there has to be an invisible connection for it to work". Bringing the mentor opportunity to new Canadians has been a highlight, and we see that organic and programmatic mentoring can be beneficial.

Ottawa Community Immigrant Services Organization (OCISO) Mentorship Program

OCISO offers mentorship opportunities to help immigrants integrate into the workforce. The program connects newcomers with established professionals in their field who provide guidance on job searches, networking, and understanding the Canadian workplace.[6]

These organizations provide valuable resources to help new immigrants navigate the challenges of settling in Canada, offering both career-focused and social support. There are many more out there!

Specific industries also have member-based associations that will provide support and resources to members, and sometimes include the bonus of mentorship programs. I've mentioned a few throughout the book, and list a few examples here.

Human Resources Professional Association (Ontario, Canada)

If you are in HR in Ontario, you might benefit from the mentor program of the Human Resources Professional Association (HRPA).[7] The HRPA mentorship program has impacted thousands of HR professionals. As I mentioned earlier, I was the Chair for my chapter for several years, and this program moved from Chapter-specific mentorship to Ontario-wide mentorship online. This allowed mentors and mentees to connect beyond their local community. Both programs worked well so long as there was the commitment and key ingredients I mentioned earlier in the book. The HRPA recently moved its formal program housed on MentorCity to a more organic platform so we will have to see if it continues to be successful. Either way, connecting with other members can lead to meaningful long-term mentorship outside of your specific company.

American Marketing Association (AMA)

The American Marketing Association (AMA) also has a reputable mentorship program.[8] You'll be more at ease with someone who has some lived experience similar to yours or a career path that you want to follow. The program it currently offers has a paid educational component, which does not necessarily align with my vision of mentorship (no cost but time). The AMA Toronto Mentor Exchange

Program scientifically matches mid-to-senior level marketing professionals with seasoned C-suite mentors, professionals in advertising, communications, marketing, market research, marketing technology or media. This is by application only. If you're lucky your organization may pay for this as additional professional development.

There are many other associations for industry-specific organizations and you can check to see if they have a mentorship program. Depending on what industry you are in, these organizations may offer mentorship programs, such as, the Canadian Nurses Association, Canadian Association for Business Economics and the Canadian Bar Association, and many more wherever you are in the world, each tailoring programs to their specific sectors. These programs often use online platforms to connect experienced professionals with mentees for guidance on career development, skill-building, and navigating professional challenges. They are typically available to members and may have specific eligibility criteria, such as membership status or work experience.

One of my clients had a member-based organization that offered mentorship programs to its members (akin to an internship) and they also offered up speed mentoring and coaching at their annual conference.

Canadian Media Producers Association (CMPA)

In 2025, the CMPA celebrated 30 years of mentorship. In a press release, the CEO, Reynolds Mastin, stated that "CMPA mentees have gone on to run companies, serve on the CMPA Board of Directors, and achieve incredible success, strengthening Canada's cultural presence on the world stage". The program is run through the support of CMPA member companies and their many industry partners, who invest in the next generation of producers.

The CMPA Mentorship Program is dedicated to bringing together emerging and established producers through on-the-job placement programs at CMPA member companies nationwide.[9] Mentees receive hands-on experience in all areas of production, including development, financing, distribution, and post-production. The program has continued to evolve to meet the changing needs of the industry. I sat down with the COO, Liz Shorten, about her experience mentoring and as she reflected on her first mentor experiences and career, the one common element is her belief that the key to success was about building authentic relationships.

After Liz graduated from Queen's University she worked in retail and sporting goods for several years and was trying to determine where to go next. She shared a story about meeting a woman in the film and television industry who took a chance on her, and how this became her first experience of being mentored. Liz was able to evolve her skills and move through the company almost as though it was a "mini film school". She will never forget how this opportunity of support and mentorship changed her career trajectory and 25 years later she remains in the industry.

Since then, she had a number of mentors, mainly women, and also started a program with another colleague, Women in View, where they created safe spaces for "ask me anything" connections— for early career women to ask questions of more experienced women leaders. This initiative was started to address some of the systemic barriers to entry into film for women. And now the CMPA and Liz are continuing to address other systemic challenges in the industry for equity seeking groups and they continue to shape the industry to reflect the communities in Canada.

The mentorship program at CMPA has evolved substantially since its inception 30 years ago, with funding model changes to allow for greater representation and diversity. They also introduced the Star Producer Program, with a curricula-based group mentorship and coaching approach and brought mentees together with their Jump Start program held at their annual conference Prime Time. This is how we see the ripple effect of mentorship in action.

Check out your local associations to see whether they offer up mentorship, you will change lives with the gift of connection, wisdom and contribution.

Choose Someone You're Comfortable With

You also need to ensure that you are comfortable and connect with the person who mentors you. As mentioned earlier, I recommend you meet a few people before deciding. As Zahra suggests above, make sure there is chemistry and you feel comfortable. Psychological safety is becoming something extremely important in mentorship relationships (and the workplace more broadly). We need to create safe spaces for mentoring and comfortable dialogue opportunities.

Sim Ozel, an experienceced talent leader, confirms this, saying mentees should choose someone they enjoy talking with and are at ease with. They should be open, drive the process and be committed. Sim also shared that while she understood the value of internal mentors as they know the context and environment, there is more freedom with an external mentor. She also believes that a mentor is often someone who inspires you.

Noreen Reid, Partner at Deloitte, has been blessed to be part of companies that offer robust and varied mentor programs, including IBM and Deloitte. Her advice for a person starting out their career who is not part of a company program is also to seek out someone they can be comfortable with. "Don't pick a mentor because they are at a certain level in a company," says Noreen. "Pick someone you think you can have an easy relationship with. If it's not natural in that mentorship, pick someone else."

Rebecca Wellum, Compliance Executive, recommends you find someone you connect with who has opinions you respect, and then listen and leverage and learn from other people's mistakes. If someone says to save yourself the energy, then why would you go about doing it anyway? Why put yourself through that kind of heartache and agony if it isn't going to benefit you? Do something that will bypass those problems, and you only learn that by listening to other people. Rebecca is always open to being a mentor. As she says "Always and Forever. I have as much to learn from others as I have to teach, and I'm determined to share, share, share until no one wants to hear what I have to say." I'd say that is another fantastic example of the ripple effect of mentorship making waves!

And as George Gettas says, "I collect energy. I look for energy that appeals to me. I am looking for people that have the same level of energy that I have. The mentor relationship succeeded because we were vibrating at the same level." For him the energy has to be right, and I agree.

So much of choosing the right mentor and mentee relationship is about the Mentor with Heart™ approach that I developed, and share as part of our programs.

Choose Someone You Admire

Another common theme that came up in my interviews is that you should choose someone you admire, or a role model who is a few steps ahead of you. For example, I had an HR mentee who was thinking about law school, so one of the reasons she reached out to me through our HRPA mentor program was that I had a Masters in Labour and Employment law and had practised law for several years. She resonated with this, and we had an excellent mentor relationship, based on common career paths and respect for one another.

The first person I interviewed for the book was a colleague I immensely admired. Cindy Bush, CHRO, and I worked together for years at CIBC and then she went on to move up in the HR field and eventually reached the CHRO level. She had a number of mentors throughout her career journey both within her organization and outside it. She says that often you probably already know who that person is. Think about that person you respect, admire, and who influences you—a person whose life and career lessons you want to understand and learn from. You probably already know who that person is, and it takes two minutes of your time to formalize that. You have to make the decision to approach them and set up the meetings. You have to be the one that puts that framework in place.

Julie Bednarski, Founder of the Healthy Crunch Company, had a similar message. She says you should look for someone you like and strive to emulate. But if that person is unable to mentor you, then find someone in the industry that is close to how you want to be, and where you want to go next. She had both mentors and coaches as she grew her business. I first met Julie when she was creating kale chips in her own kitchen, and now she has many lines of healthy snacks, and is ready to give to the next generation of entrepreneurs. I admired Julie's strong belief in self, and this internal guidance can lead you to the right support. So as a mentee, know what you really want and go after it.

"How do you go about this? I would say LinkedIn. You have to go out there and ask lots of people for help. Ask questions. You have to have that confidence, to go out and do that."— *Julie Bednarski*

Mario McCracken, a sales leader and expert, says the same. One thing he realized when looking for good mentors was to choose someone he wanted to be like and ask himself how he could help them. He says if you find that person and discover how to help them, then the mentor-mentee relationship will take off naturally. It has to be reciprocal, otherwise the other person won't be invested. It's hard to be invested in something if you don't care. The best way to get them to care is to help them and serve them and be there for them and they'll notice your abilities and realize you are someone they can put themselves behind.

So, all in all, we all say "Go for it!"—and so did Natalie Dumond Leadership Coach. Natalie is another proponent of believing in yourself enough, knowing that you are worthy to also receive whatever you desire. As a Dare to Lead certified coach she has coached and mentored many and she encourages you to simply find someone on LinkedIn that inspires you and send them a direct message or an email. Most people do want to pay it forward and help others.

Hopefully by now you have the confidence to go out there and find that person and reach out. One day you might be the one that someone admires and respects. It is all about continuing that ripple effect of giving through mentorship.

Determine the Right Match

Now that you have narrowed down your potential mentors, how do you decide which one is the best match for you? The right mentor should be someone you trust, respect, and who shares your values. These three things are important, because they will dictate the strength and trajectory of the relationship.

Finding the right fit, chemistry or connection is critical to the future success of the relationship. Sarah Shu says to "Stress the right fit for mentor and mentee. The mentor and/or the coach needs to believe in you and see the potential that you're not able to see at the moment." Sarah and I started some mentor/coach circles years ago after we met through Coralus (formerly SheEO). We experimented with giving our knowledge back to others.

> "What is the right mentor fit for you? Consider their experience, their style, their availability—that's a big one. Interview a few before you choose. It's okay to have different mentors and coaches for different aspects of your life."— *Eva Marie Moffatt*

I also recommend that you meet with a number of potential mentors before you dive into a commitment and a lengthy relationship with them. As Eva Marie said, it should also be like interviewing for a role at an organization—who do you want to spend this time with?

I spoke about this approach earlier when talking about mentors within your organization, and it should be the same for external mentor relationships.

I also met with Lisa Da Rocha, a leadership coach, who had some great advice for those looking for a mentor. Lisa said to look less at what someone has accomplished from an external perspective. Look for someone you connect with, someone you can trust, someone you can be your real self with. Your gut will tell you when this is the person you need to be with.

Lisa believes that too often people look for a mentor who is at the top of their game and that is not, in most cases, the person that you're supposed to be with or the person that's going to help you the most. When people approach Lisa about mentoring them, she has an interesting question she asks them all: "Have you met with anyone else?" She tells them they need to meet with at least two other people because they don't know what kind of connection they have until they can compare it to something. She also applies this to her coaching practice.

"I might be a *hell yes!* when you meet me—and after meeting a couple of other people, I might not be the mentor for you."— *Lisa Da Rocha*

This approach of meeting more than one person before deciding was also confirmed by Carol Schulte, a motivational speaker and coach. Carol has overcome so many obstacles and challenges in her life and inspires me to be braver! She advises exploring a few different options but ultimately finding someone who resonates with you and your values. Don't be unduly influenced by how successful they are or appear to be, but whether or not you feel comfortable with them and feel open and honest and authentic with them. An authentic relationship is what makes a good partnership, and not everybody works the same way.

In her speaking engagements, Carol advises her audiences they need to find someone who thinks as they do. If you find someone who focuses on the internal game and the soft skills you need and that's what you're about, great. If you have someone who is business savvy and knows the numbers, and you're very much driven and ambitious like that, then work with that person.

"What works on you is what will work for you."—*Carol Schulte*

All of these sentiments can be applied to traditional no-cost mentorship as well as finding paid coaches who have a mentor approach of teaching and giving.

The theme of trust also came up quite a bit in my interviews, and all generations seemed to agree on this as an important component of an ideal mentorship. Denise Allison, a digital marketing expert, says you should look for someone who knows what you're going through and someone who has had similar challenges so that they can guide you through it. A mentor should be someone you trust, and someone who drives with you. If you don't like someone's approach, they might be great, but maybe not the best for you.

Edita Atteck, Coach, Author and Founder of Khalix, skin-care products and community, says before you determine the best mentor for you, look inward. "Just knowing your inner gut feeling and knowing who you can trust. Any kind of advancement and any kind of learning can only happen in a place where your nervous system is letting go of guards and you really feel protected." I met Edita as part of a community years ago and admire how grounded she is and with her inner wisdom. I explored my creative side with her and learned a lot from her over the years. Sometimes the mentor may not even realize they are one!

Reiterating the need to find the right match, it's important to have that connection and both be committed, says Elizabeth Williams whom you met earlier in the book.

> "At the end of the day we need to connect as human beings, and if we can't form a connection then it's time to walk away. It's like dating in that sense—just swipe left and keep going. That's fundamental—you need to like and trust each other."— *Elizabeth Williams*

Set Up the Meeting and Ask the Right Questions
Once you've taken some of the advice above, networked, had some coffee chats, followed people and commented on their posts, it's time to decide who you want to mentor you.

You know who is the right mentor for this point in your life and career so now it's time to commit to it.

After you've built a relationship with your potential ideal mentor and you've gained your confidence and clarity, you need to meet again and ask if they'd be willing to commit to a formal mentorship.

When you meet a potential mentor, there are three things you should know about them:

- their availability
- their experience
- their leadership/mentorship style

Before you select your mentor, it's important to determine if they are available to participate in a mentorship, as they might already be mentoring someone else or don't have the time to dedicate to becoming a mentor. They need to decide they have a connection with you as well.

Making the time and commitment to mentorship is challenging with the pace of life and work. Yet once both people commit it will be an unforgettable experience.

You have a world of growing ahead of you, and some day you'll also mentor others and start that ripple effect.

Good luck—and please reach out to me with your mentorship stories or questions any time by sending a note to helen@lifework swell.ca.

Our newest Life Works Well project, *One Million Mentor Moments*, explores the ripple effect of mentoring in the way I describe in this book. If you'd like to know more about this movement and how you might participate, send me an email with "One Million Mentor Moments" in the subject line, visit our website or tag us on social media.

Now let's take a look at how we may go further to create a mentor culture in the community and the world.

10

———————

CREATE A MENTOR WORLD

"Mentorship is about planting seeds of possibility. The greatest legacy isn't what we teach, but the trust and hope we nurture in others." —*Leigh Mitchell*

My dream is for us to live in a mentor world, one where there are *Everyday Mentors*©, and where giving and receiving is embedded in workplaces, communities and the world. Can you envision such a world? I believe it can happen through a ripple effect, and leaders who provide time for mentorship inside and outside of their organizations will see the impact in action.

I call this *Mentor In and Mentor Out* © . Throughout this book, I've focused mainly on how to create a mentor culture within your organization, and now I'd like to open up a discussion on what it could mean to mentor outside of the organization itself and how this might work. This can be linked to your volunteerism strategy and corporate social responsibility initiatives.

Mentoring Out/Corporate Social Responsibility

The idea of connection, and bringing back meaningful deep relationships, has been on my mind for some time. I believe living through the COVID-19 pandemic changed the world of work on both a collective and intimate level. As humans, we realized we can't keep living the way we have been.

The world experienced an awakening, a realization that healing is required. We began to acknowledge that we as humans are connected, our energy is intertwined and one of the best ways to be alive is to be in community or relationship with others.

We saw that we were missing that deep human connection in the way we were living our lives.

If you want to be part of the change that is inevitably coming, what better way to reconnect than to mentor others inside your company, in your community and globally?

As I researched the world of mentoring, I discovered the Global Mentorship Initiative. I've also been working in partnership with other companies here in Canada, including MentorCity and Black Mentorship Inc. We all have a common purpose—to bring true connection back into the world. Having mentorship as part of a work and community culture is key to unlocking potential for everyone.

What does the term "culture" mean to you?

For some, it is their family of origin background, where they came from, or their heritage. This has now been carried over into organizations, and employers believe their cultures are unique. Dr. Nava Israel in her compelling book *Conetrolled* defines culture as "everything I and the group I am affiliated with consider true and normal. There are mini cultures in organizations and communities and it can be as few as two people."[1] Leaders who understand the importance of creating sustainable, healthy and heart-centered cultures will succeed. Creating a mentor culture inside and outside the organization is also part of this.

By my definition, culture in a workplace is a shared set of beliefs and behaviours that provide the organization and its employees with a sense of purpose, vision and guidance. Purpose-driven companies who are truly committed to sustainability and Environmental, Social and Governance (ESG) goals will sustain in the long run. A focus on human relations (my vision of HR) is what will help them stand out. An important aspect of this connection is mentorship and embedding it as part of the fabric of the company is what will "create a mentor culture".

Let's review some of the incredible organizations out there starting a ripple effect of mentorship.

Global Mentorship Initiative (GMI)

Global Mentorship Initiative (GMI) is helping create this link for new graduates starting out their career. (While this is wonderful it also needs to start earlier. Fortunately, there are other organizations who are also making this happen.)

Every student deserves a champion. One person to guide them as they navigate the transition from college to career. Through a structured, online, one-to-one mentorship with a business professional, we are connecting students to employment, transforming communities, and building a brighter tomorrow.[2]

They are building an ecosystem to empower a generation of students around the world through partnerships with companies and educational institutions. This is one way to create a mentor culture inside and outside the organization.

An organization can connect employees with university and college students and build the relationship for future employees in a creative way through mentorship.

I spoke with the Founder of GMI, Jon Browning, and his passion and vision is incredible. In the last five years, GMI has impacted over 9,000 students and refugees to help them launch their careers. Jon believes that if you help a young person get the right start in life, anything is possible. He believes in the power of mentorship to transform lives and in our journey we can reflect on how others helped us reach our goals. We can give back and provide support to people who may not have the same privileges.

My vision is very much aligned to that of GMI. This is the ripple effect of mentorship in action. When we receive mentorship and guidance, we will in turn mentor others. As the student is mentored by the teacher, they in turn will pass their own knowledge and guidance on to others. This is how the ripple starts and continues. And this is an amazing example of how to mentor with heart.

Junior Achievers

Another way to connect your volunteerism program to mentoring is to allow employees time off to mentor in the community of your office locations. At ADP Canada, for example, we partnered with Junior Achievers to volunteer in the local elementary schools, helping children learn financial acumen. Training and time off were provided to do this.

Junior Achievers (JA) has been around since 1955, and they have educated and inspired over five million young Canadians. JA prepares students to succeed and gives them knowledge and confidence in school, business and life.

JA volunteers include individual professionals who sign up through their organizations' JA volunteer programs. Volunteers generously donate their time to inspire Canadian youth as they prepare for their future.

These dedicated volunteers facilitate programs for students in grades three to twelve to teach them about financial literacy, work readiness and entrepreneurship. Topics include learning to create a budget, developing long-term goals, understanding what it takes to run a successful business,and learning about different types of investments and payment methods. JA provides training, support and program materials to ensure volunteers have a fun and meaningful experience.

What a great way for employees to give back through this type of early years mentorship! Of course, this can also be applied to other skill sets that will help youth gain confidence and hope for the future.

Starting mentorship at a young age has been shown to impact the success of the student in life, as discussed in this 2018 article by Jennifer Jones-Morales and Alison M. Konrad.[3]

The study tracked the success of students of primary school age who had early mentors, and who thrived as a result. If your organization can provide paid time off, and work with an organization like JA or others, it will help create the ripple effect I envision.

Many resources can be found on the JA website.[4]

Mentor Canada

Mentor Canada[5] is a Canadian non-profit organization originally affiliated with Big Brothers and Sisters. They say there are currently over 15,000 young Canadians looking for mentorship.

Mentoring requires an open mind and an interest in making a difference in the life of a young person. You can volunteer once a week or once a month, so the time commitment is up to you. Mentor Canada's website contains more resources.

I met with the former executive director of Mentor Canada, Stacey Dakin, who said that anyone can have a mentor mindset. This is something I also call the Everyday Mentor© and is about creating one-off mentor moments in your company, community and the world.

Mentor Canada also conducts research and provides studies and data to support the need for this. Of young people who are mentored, 53% are more likely to report good or excellent mental health, over twice as likely to complete high school, and 95% are more likely to have pursued further education after high school.

Mentor National

Mentor National[6] is an organization in the U.S. that leads, expands, and strengthens the mentoring movement, building capacity to make high-quality relationships accessible to all young people. I have been following this organization for years and love their mission and vision as it aligns with mine. Mentor Canada worked with this organization and Big Brothers and Sisters to bring similar concepts to life. They help grassroots organization through their research in the field, shaping policy and advocacy and creating public awareness for the value of mentorship.

I met with the previous CEO, David Shapiro, about his passion for mentorship. David decided early in his career to support others given his privilege, and he had access to witness how mentorship worked within the sports scene and in the real world. He mentored a young man through Big Brothers and Sisters and decades later they have a beautiful relationship.

While a lot of his work in philanthropy and non-profits included mentorship, he sees that what we call these relationships, or the terminology we use, doesn't necessarily matter as much. He talked about what was more important is the "covenant" you make with each other—structure it so the two participants can be successful living the covenant out. Whether we are sponsors, mentors, friends, coaches, the intention behind our commitment and covenant is what truly matters. Whether we care and support is what makes the difference. Intentionality is what makes it work, our commitment, consistency in showing up for someone who needs us—not in the form of saviourism or "I know better". I loved our conversation and believe that at the core is the "mentor with heart" concept of giving without expectation, with unconditional love and care.

Black Mentorship Inc.

One organization I admire is Black Mentorship Inc. (BMI), which was founded by Evangeline Chima in 2020 in the midst of the global COVID-19 pandemic. This happened before the George Floyd murder and the heightened focus on equity, diversity and inclusion in organizations. There was a gap and need, and Evangeline saw it, informed by her own experiences and discrimination she faced in the workplace. The focus on justice and anti-racism for the Black community has helped highlight the need for organizations like BMI.

BMI is dedicated to the empowerment of Black Professionals in Canada. It creates leadership opportunities by connecting Black youth, professionals and entrepreneurs at different stages of professional growth with industry experts through their unique mentoring programs. BMI exists to elevate professional advancement through mentorship, education, and skill building, thus building a better, more equitable workforce.[7]

BMI's mentorship program aims to bridge the gap and mentor access within the Black and Black, Indigenous, and People of Color (BIPOC) professional community. This organization is dedicated to addressing these challenges by providing an inclusive mentorship program to enhance the growth, empowerment and career development of Black people. As well as education and skill building, they also provide resources, networking and strong community support to enable participants to achieve their definition of success, eradicating systemic barriers and creating diverse leaders.

Your company can find an organization like BMI to provide mentorship, time and resources to help create a mentor world. This is the linkage I envision with creating mentor programs in your organization, but also providing time off or volunteer hours for employees to give back in their community to organizations like BMI or other non-profits.

When I spoke with Evangeline about her journey, both in work and life, she mentioned that her greatest success comes from being true to herself. When things are hard, she looks for people who can support her and her ongoing growth. When she decided to start BMI, her vision was to have a space for others to find someone who represents them, a gap that wasn't available to her in the organizations she worked with in Canada. Mentorship is part of her everyday life, many people approached her for career advice and she was encouraged by others to create mentoring and coaching programs.

Mentoring has always been part of Evangeline, giving her knowledge, time and resources. She believes that one of the most important aspects is to create a safe, nurturing and comfortable environment, especially for one-on-one mentor relationships. Trust may not be built immediately in a three- or six-month program, it takes time, and ideally meaningful life time relationships will be built over time. It is not necessary though to have connection from the beginning. If you have a clear "Why" then that is the focus and you can get that with or without connection. I found this an interesting perspective. For Black professionals, we also need to remember that their lived experiences are much different than those of us who are privileged.

While our backgrounds may differ, Evangeline and I had a similar experience in that the organizations we worked with didn't communicate the mentor and sponsorship programs or opportunity well. It was not available to us, and in Evangeline's words she received "zero, nada, none"! I'm sure some of us can relate to this. And yet, the experience for Black professionals remains more difficult. That's why BMI was born, so that others did not have to feel this way. BMI has grown immensely since I first met Evangeline and is continuing to make an impact, the mentorship ripple effect in action! If you'd like to implement a mentor program for your Black professionals, contact BMI. As an individual, if you are able to support this organization, through donations, sponsorship or becoming a mentor or an ally, I encourage you to do so!

Mentoring in the entrepreneur world

For those who have their own business, or are exploring self--employment, an entire world of entrepreneurship is available. Mentorship is available through organizations such as Futurpreneur and Start Up Canada (and Start Up Women) and many more globally. I've been a mentor for both organizations and it has been an incredible experience. These programs provide the opportunity for the mentor/mentee to connect for one meeting or a series, and I met so many incredible young entrepreneurs. Being a mentor brought me immense joy, and inspired me as much as my advice and guidance helped the mentees. If you have entrepreneurial experience, you could provide volunteer time for this. As little as one hour per month will make an impact on future generations.

In addition to Mentor Canada, (and Mentor National in the U.S.), it's a good idea to find a local organization in the community where your employees live. Or better yet, let your employees be part of deciding how to give back in this way.[6]

MentorCity

MentorCity[8] is an organization that provides mentorship through their free global mentorship option. In addition, they have clients in both corporate for-profit and non-profit organizations.

I met Shawn Mintz, the President and founder of MentorCity as Shawn's platform was the one used by the Human Resources Professional Association in Ontario (HRPA) for the last decade. The HRPA has over 25,000 HR members, and mentorship is a key part of their membership offer.

I was chair of mentorship for the West Toronto Chapter for several years, and enhanced their program by offering education sessions on group mentoring, how to be a great mentor and more. We increased the number of mentor pairings year over year, and took interest in the mentorship program to the next level.

Organizations that allow employees the space and time to give back through volunteerism are sought after by top talent. And those that also offer mentoring to employees are amazing places to work and sought after by new employees. Gen Z expects to learn and grow and be mentored, as well as opportunities to give back. There are many associations who need volunteers, and this could also be an opportunity to mentor out.

Shawn and his team help implement the mentor programs, providing tools that are right for each organization. Having a platform that can help track success with video options and community capability is so important to the success of the initiative. It helps to deepen connections across all mentorship pairings.

Shawn's free mentor program is how I first found out about

MentorCity, while researching various platforms and the world of mentorship. This was a new experience using this platform, and my first mentor relationship using this service was with a fellow in the UK, and while it was a short time period, it made me realize the incredible opportunity that mentoring around the world can provide, connecting virtually through technology. I've now used this technology with a few organizations and it is an easy-to-use tool. While Shawn works with many companies who implement mentor programs using this platform, offering a free service is a wonderful way to contribute and make an impact.

> "I think that we need to do more of this to create a true MentorCity —a place that encourages all people living in our communities to reach their potential. Everyone has something valuable to share and by sharing your experiences, you are providing one of the greatest gifts of insight and knowledge. It starts with a few minutes of your time and can turn into one of the most enriching experiences in your life."—*Shawn Mintz*

Shawn started his career in the non-profit sector in marketing and communications and during that time he worked with new Canadians and started mentoring there. He had an idea in 2011 (to create his company) and asked his mentors what they thought about it. They thought it was fantastic and it gave him the confidence to develop his business plan and hasn't looked back since.

He believes that anything is possible and stays true to his vision and where he wants to go. One of his favourite mentor experiences was supporting a mentee in the software business, passing on encouragement, guidance and cheering him on! Connection and commonality can help build the foundation and trust as the relationship evolves. Like many I met with, he sees benefit in both formal and informal mentorship, and loves working with clients who see the positive outcomes that come from mentor programs in their organization.

Shawn wrote a guide on mentorship, *How a few minutes with the right person can change your life*, which provides valuable tips on mentoring and highlights four types of mentors—Networking, Career, Project and Personal Mentors. In addition to implementing the platform in companies, he provides training and education on how to be successful in mentor programs and how to measure the return on investment. I've learned so much from Shawn and consider him one of my "everyday mentors". To learn more, you can also review our mentor circle with Shawn on the Life Works Well resource portal.

Ten Thousand Coffees (now 10KC.com)

The organization Ten Thousand Coffees (10KC.com)[9] has evolved in the mentorship space since 2014, and they are on a mission to "democratize opportunity for all, and have fun while they do it!"

Back in 2014, Ten Thousand Coffees co-founder Dave Wilkin, former CEO, and Elliott Garcia, then CTO, spoke with several CEOs and Fortune 500 leaders on the subject of talent development. It turned out that informal conversations among colleagues provided the best learning and career development opportunities, and the most inclusive cultures.

They also found that because of their informal nature, these experiences were not only left to chance, but were not measurable. They were usually people chatting over lunch or in common work areas, which is not easy to quantify.

There was also the problem of unconscious bias, which resulted in preferential treatment that left under-represented groups with fewer informal development opportunities.

Dave and Elliott saw the need to improve on the foundation of these informal conversations, and Ten Thousand Coffees was established.

"Human connections are at the core of career development, culture, innovation, and inclusion. We built Ten Thousand Coffees to create meaningful connections at scale."—*Dave Wilkin*

The company eventually evolved and now you can be matched to professionals through 10KC.com's more than 80 private mentoring and networking communities at Canadian universities and colleges.[10]

10KC.com provides many resources on its website.

I had the opportunity to sit down with the co-founder, Dave Wilkin, when I was interviewing for the book. Dave's journey is incredibly moving, as he grew up as a gay kid in a rural small-town community, and this was the genesis for his passion for mentorship. He learned at a very young age that if you didn't have mentors or networks, you didn't receive any opportunities. Having experienced being treated differently, everything was simply harder. If it wasn't for a full scholarship, Dave would not have been able to experience post-secondary education at Waterloo.

Dave studied bio-chemistry, and thought he would become a doctor. He then went to an entrepreneurship conference (he knew nothing about it), where he saw a speaker from a rural Northern town even smaller than his. This speaker inspired him and he approached her with the intent of landing a job; she encouraged him to start his first company, became his mentor and years later they remain very close.

Dave had started several non-profits and at 18 years old he spoke on behalf of the government at organizations to help high-light the importance of mentorship and the future of work. What Dave and his co-founder decided was that if they combined the online dating technology with a learning and development system, they could change the world of mentoring. And the rest is history! It started as online dating for mentors in 2014, and after testing for years, they saw the impact, and so did organizations who approached them to bring mentor matching inside their compa-nies. More recently the enterprise evolved to include sponsorship programs and diversity, inclusion and belonging has always been a central tenet of the vision. Their system includes networking, mentoring, coaching and sponsorship modules and they are all connected, and especially important for supporting equity seeking groups within any company. What I also love about 10KC.com is that their giving back strategy includes support to social impact organizations who could use the system at no cost or very low cost. This is the mentor ripple effect and mentoring with heart in action!

There are many software platforms out there now, and many of them have a giving back component, and then there are other organizations who focus not only on technology, but the beauty of mentorship itself.

Center for Mentoring Excellence

Years ago, I came across a book called Bridging Differences for Better Mentoring, co-written by Dr. Lois J. Zachary and her daughter Lisa Fain. I attended an online webinar when they were reintroducing an updated version of it. That was my solidification that I was on the right path and that the more people that spread the value of mentorship the better.

It wasn't until much later that this led me to eventually meeting Lisa, the CEO of the Center for Mentoring Excellence, and she has inspired me to continue my path. I am happy to have met her, and consider her a role model and a mentor. We both lost our mothers in the same year and have a similar background having been lawyers, and passionate about justice and equity, diversity, inclusion and belonging.

Her journey to mentorship started while in law when a women's employee resource group wanted a mentoring program. She consulted with her mother, Dr. Lois Zachary, who was the founder of Center for Mentoring Excellence at that time and they came in to help them kick off the program. As Lisa's mom was presenting, she had a realization that the power of mentoring relationships could help create more inclusive workplace cultures. A few years later, she left the corporate world and joined the Center for Mentoring Excellence. The rest is history![11]

As noted, Lisa is the co-author of Bridging Differences for Better Mentoring, and the 2022 revision (3rd Edition) of The Mentor's

Guide[12]. Both are co-authored with Center for Mentoring Excellence's original founder, Dr. Lois J. Zachary.

Through her work as the CEO of Center for Mentoring Excellence, she has conducted mentoring training programs for corporate, government and educational institutions. Lisa coaches mentors, mentees, and program administrators on how to achieve mentoring excellence and create the right environment for achievement of career and personal goals. She is also the President of the International Mentoring Association and these organizations continue to help create the ripple effect of mentorship.

Lisa has been both a mentor and coach, and been mentored by her mother and in her legal career. She believes that as mentors we can learn so much from our mentees and gain as much or more from the relationship. She says "All good mentors are coaches (though not all coaches are mentors)", and will continue to mentor in the future.

Twomentor

Twomentor is a high-impact management consulting company focused on building a happier, more productive, and inclusive workforce. Founded by Julie Kantor, Twomentor works with corporations, higher education, professional associations, and non-profits. Julie has become one of my "everyday mentors" and I've been inspired by her for a few years now.

She is a champion for mentorship and sponsorship, and Twomentor works as an extended part of the team to build and manage sustainable employee engagement and retention initiatives. Many of the organizations they work with understand the value of mentorship and they have created many valuable white papers[13]. Many companies do not have the internal bandwidth or expertise to effectively manage their program, and like Life Works Well, Twomentor operates as an extension of the team, providing dynamic mentorship, and sponsorship programs aligned with an organization's unique needs.

Julie and I hit it off immediately, as our passion for mentorship and our parents' life journeys had a lot of parallels. Julie has trained thousands of mentor program managers on how to implement successful mentor programs. Prior to founding Twomentor, she worked for 20 years with the Network for Teaching Entrepreneurship where she created mentorship and sponsor programs. This vision aligns with the mentor out concept, as much of the need is beyond the private corporations. She believes in always paying it forward, and when we work with corporate leaders with heart, they get mentorship. Julie is someone I now consider a reciprocal mentor and an inspiration to me! The "power of two" concept makes so much sense.

National Mentoring Day

I was also fortunate to meet and interview Chelsey Baker, a global leader in Mentoring. She has worked on leading government mentoring projects and has mentored thousands of start-up businesses. Chelsey is also the founder of a non-profit in the UK and started National Mentoring Day, now a global movement[14]! National Mentoring Day started in 2014 and takes place every October 27th and was inaugurated in the Houses of Parliament. Part of the initiative is One Person One Hour, encouraging people around the globe to mentor one person for one hour on this day. The goal is to make mentoring accessible for all. This is truly a Mentor with Heart™ ripple effect in action

The initiative is now the largest celebration of mentoring with over 250,000 organisations around the world taking part each year to celebrate the impact of mentoring across enterprise, education and communities and supporting all forms of mentoring, aimed to shine a light on mentors and mentoring initiatives making an impact.

Our visions aligned, and Chelsey and I clicked instantly, and we both said "where have all the mentors gone?" They are the only organization in the world that supports mentoring and mentor programs exclusively and what I also loved is that Chelsey links mentorship as a way to help address all of the UN's Sustainable Development Goals (SDGs). Again, we are so aligned as this is part of the vision of Mentor

In Mentor Out™ and moving to make a difference beyond the typical corporation. Chelsey says "Mentoring is the antidote to the world's greatest business, educational and social challenges. Mentoring works across every sector, every industry, across every border, every language and every circumstance. Mentoring has no age, no borders. People are struggling, loneliness is spreading and just one word, one sentence, just your presence, just showing up, just listening is often enough."

When Chelsey and I spoke, we realized we both had a similar story in relation to not having mentors throughout our life. She also felt the need to close that gap for others and created the largest celebration of mentoring in the world. The ripple effects are massive! For her, mentoring is passing on your skills, experience, wisdom and perspective to help shape someone else's life, career or business and help them to grow, flourish and develop on their own. Chelsey mentors in the experience that she has, and for her that is 25 years in media, PR and television and publishing and that is the beauty of it. She has used this skillset and wisdom to create National Mentoring Day, the marketing machine for mentorship throughout the world. They have hundreds of resources to help organizations amplify their mentoring messages. I can't wait to see where Chelsey and I take our passion and belief in mentorship in the future!

UGO Impact and Sabbaticals

If your organization can provide paid or unpaid sabbaticals linked to mentorship or volunteering at a non-profit or NGO (or abroad), this is a wonderful way to give back. It's all part of creating a mentor world.

UGO Impact[15], founded by Jill Valentine, offers transformative travel combined with volunteerism and life coaching. She is a pioneer in the transformational travel arena. Jill had the brilliant idea to harness the innate power of coaching, travel and volunteerism after becoming a Certified Professional Coach and then spending a month in the Philippines helping to rebuild after Typhoon Yolanda.

With this powerful combination, Jill now provides coaching

clients with the clarity, confidence and community to create personal and social change, while at the same time impacting communities in need around the world.

Jill is the creator of The UGO Triple Change Effect Model which inspires individuals to clarify their life purpose, step into their full power and change their world. She recently created her Give and Grow community in the greater Toronto area, which will widely spread the effect of volunteering in the community and personal self-development.

I met Jill through Women in Biz Network (WIBN), an organization founded by Leigh Mitchell (whom you'll meet next). Jill serves to inspire and encourage, and understands the struggle to find more meaning in life. Although always feeling a call to service, Jill didn't feel a deep and fulfilling sense of purpose until the age of 32, despite years in the charity sector. She now meshes a passion to serve others, travel and community building to transform clients' lives and the communities they visit.

Jill has led programs in Belize, Nepal, Costa Rica, Puerto Rico and Tanzania and has a talent for creating safe, intimate spaces for clients to comfortably volunteer abroad, journey within and create deep bonds with one another. I am also part of Jill's Give and Grow Community for locals to gather to give back, volunteer and connect in meaningful ways and it has been extremely fulfilling.

In late 2022 I decided to travel abroad with Jill to Tanzania, Africa on one of her trips. This experience further deepened my commitment to contribution and I grew in many ways. We volunteered with Dare to Lead run by Maggie Duncan and started to build a shelter for women and children fleeing domestic violence. Spending time with the "mamas" and seeing how Maggie is helping women become independent through mentorship, guidance and support was incredible.

I also climbed Mt. Kilimanjaro, which is something I never had on a bucket list and never thought I could accomplish at the age of 59! This truly was a life-changing experience, getting out of my comfort zone and believing that anything is possible no matter what age or stage of life you're in. I wrote a piece on LinkedIn, where I talked about "awakening" in Tanzania. This experience reminded me that we can be mentors every day. We supported each other as a group on that mountain. When one of us didn't think we could go on, we encouraged and motivated one another, with Jill leading the way. We gave each other strength and courage, and this allowed me to transcend myself in a period of difficult physical and mental challenge. Mentorship doesn't always need to be through a program, it can be in the tough times and good times, and is always available.

Applying this attitude to mentorship and volunteerism will transform individuals and organizations. Imagine the impact on your organization if you were to provide this type of unpaid or paid leave for your employees to give back!

You can also support a non-profit or charitable organization with your employees' time and service by setting up a paid sabbatical. To create this type of program, you'll need a process to decide which charitable or social impact organizations your company wants to support through monetary donations, volunteer time, mentorship and/or a paid exchange of services.

The employee would work for six months, the minimum needed to make an impact. They would help the non-profit or charitable organization set up various operational or other programs by providing expertise with minimal cost. This is a huge opportunity to give back through mentorship and guidance in your community or globally.

ChangeMaker Collective

Leigh Mitchell is a Brand Marketing Consultant I met many years ago, and we connected over our shared passion for mentorship. We have a reciprocal mentoring relationship, which has blossomed into a lifelong professional partnership and friendship. Leigh is a passionate leader and mentor, known for her impactful work with the Women in Biz Network (WIBN), where she launched and led a successful six-month mentorship program called Mentor Her Biz. This program matches members with one-on-one mentors, and I was proud to be involved in further developing the program. Leigh is deeply committed to mentorship as a tool for empowerment, mental health support, and social impact, reflecting her DEI (Diversity, Equity and Inclusion) advocacy in community and workplace settings.

Leigh and I both share a passion for supporting students in post-secondary education, drawn from our own unique career paths. I joined her in her York University Digital Marketing classroom to share my advice on mentorship and career development. I also mentored many students in the classroom when I taught, and beyond. Leigh also works in other established programs in the community and workplace, such as The Prosperity Project, YSpace, YEDI, Rise and Next Stars. There are numerous options for corporations to mentor beyond the workplace.

In my work with her program, Mentor Her Biz, I served as the lead of the mentoring program, focusing on areas such as HR, law, and mentorship resources within the WIBN community. I collaborated closely with the program mentors and mentees and loved matching them and watching them flourish as the program progressed.

One of the standout mentorship success stories is with Doina Oncel, founder of hEr VOLUTION, a diversity-driven girls' STEM based organization. Doina benefited from ongoing mentorship that extended beyond the formal program, illustrating the long-term relationships the program creates. Leigh and Doina have shared their story publicly, emphasizing the value and best practices of mentoring.

Leigh has shifted the focus from working exclusively with women to a new program called the ChangeMaker Collective, which targets social impact leaders, thereby expanding her mentorship to include both male and female leaders within social enterprise organizations. Leigh's lifelong passion for advocacy is directed towards accessible mentorship, and she is dedicated to supporting both emerging and established leaders from diverse backgrounds and abilities, including newcomers to Canada and persons with disabilities. Her work champions collaboration, reciprocity, and mental health awareness, underscoring how mentorship creates crucial support networks.

Leigh's personal openness about her mental health journey fuels her belief in the power to build meaningful mentorship connections in challenging times. With the world of work rapidly changing, professionals and entrepreneurs need support more than ever. As a result, AI mentorship has been added to the list of areas in which we provide support. This may be a topic for another day! I look forward to seeing Leigh's ongoing contribution as she remains active in mentorship, teaching, community building, and supporting both emerging and established leaders from diverse backgrounds.[16]

Mental Health and Mentor Health©

Speaking at a DisruptHR event back in the fall of 2015, I quoted the stat that one in five Canadians would face mental health issues. Since the pandemic, today in 2026, that number is now one in three.

If your organization can link mentorship to better mental health in your organization, that's even better. With remote work and isolation on the rise, now more than ever virtual and in person mentoring inside and outside your organization will help keep your employees healthy. There is evolving data that links mentorship to wellbeing and being a mindful mentor will go a long way to better mental health.

Linking your corporate social responsibility initiatives and volunteerism to mentorship will create healthier workplaces and a better world. Can you imagine being part of that?

11

THE RIPPLE EFFECT OF MENTORING

"Mentorship matters. It can create ripples for years ahead, one mentor moment at a time!"—*Helen Patterson*

I first began taking a deeper interest in mentorship back in 2017. It didn't take long for me to understand its value to both the mentor and mentee, and the resulting benefits to organizations that had mentoring programs.

In this book, I've attempted to expand on my understanding of the advantages of mentorship. I also provided practical information to help organizations and individuals set up their own mentoring programs or relationships and to ensure that mentoring becomes part of their organizational DNA.

As I've shown through statistics, studies and my own experience, there is no downside to mentoring. It is beneficial to individual careers as well as corporate bottom lines. Mentoring has been shown to improve people's mental and emotional well-being as the process makes a positive impact on their careers and life.

Through the data gathered in my research and from the interviews with a broad spectrum of leaders, coaches and mentors, the overwhelming result is that mentorship matters. It can create a ripple effect when the right alignment and commitment happens.

Finally, I discussed the impact of a mentorship world being immeasurable. In these turbulent times, I believe the purposeful spreading of mentorship across the globe will move towards the creation of a kinder, more inclusive and peaceful world.

Every one of us has the power to impact another person's life by being an Everyday Mentor™, or giving some support in some way. If we look at mentorship as one way to give back, it can become a part of our personal and professional missions. It will help create spaces where organic sharing, two-way knowledge exchange and connection will make lives better.

Mentoring can happen every day, in small day-to-day exchanges and that's why I created an initiative called One Million Mentor Moments (OMMMs) through our organization Life Works Well. This project aims to normalize the act of mentorship by witnessing it in everyday moments, and spreading the joy and news through our platform. We can all use some positive news in this troubling and difficult time that we're in and ideally this book and movement can inspire people to create an even wider ripple effect on a more global and collective scale.

So many of us, me included, desire to create an impact, to contribute something meaningful to the world. Yet we don't always see it. We have little control and visibility on how we may impact people. Most people tend to believe that their impact is minimal if they are not in a position of "power". I believe this is not the truth or an accurate reflection. We are all part of this mysterious butterfly effect where we are constantly impacting each other, the ripple effect in action daily.

The question then becomes: what will the quality of your impact be?

We have to find new ways of creating goodness and impacting people positively. And for me and you, OMMMs is one of these ways. Although we are only at the beginning of this part of the journey, I know we can create new mentor moments together. I'm incredibly humbled by the stories of mentoring moments we've already received through the hashtag #OMMMs and with others sending their stories directly. Proof that it is real, happening right in front of us constantly, and it works.

Will you join me in this movement? You can start today by becoming an Everyday Mentor™, Mentoring with Heart™ and joining our One Million Mentor Moments (OMMMs) project by sharing your mentor moments with us!

NOTES

Introduction

1. *https://mentoringcanada.ca/sites/default/files/2021-04/Mapping%20the%20Gap_Exec%20Summary_ENG_4.pdf*
2. Garmire LX. Mentorship is not co-authorship: a revisit to mentorship. *Genome Biol.* 2021;22(1):2. Published 2021 Jan 4. doi:10.1186/s13059-020-02226-6 and https://www.youthmentor.org/thestats
3. https://www.mentoring.org/resource/the-mentoring-effect/ *Source: MENTOR: The National Mentoring Partnership*
4. *https://mentoringcanada.ca/sites/default/files/2021-04/Mapping%20the%20Gap_Exec%20Summary_ENG_4.pdf*
5. https://www.forbes.com/councils/forbescommunicationscouncil/2022/05/19/does-mentoring-still-matter-for-fortune-500-companies/

1. What is Mentorship and how does it differ from other supportive relationships?

1. https://www.theatlantic.com/business/archive/2017/10/the-odyssey-mentorship/542676/
2. Ibid.
3. https://mentorcanada.ca/en/knowledge/research-resources
4. https://www.pdf.net/assets/uploads/Coaching%20Islamic%20Culture%202017Chapter1.pdf
5. https://hbr.org/2019/11/the-leader-as-coach
6. https://sloanreview.mit.edu/article/getting-representative-sponsorship-right-in-your-organization/
7. Harvard Business Review Press, 2019
8. https://bhasinconsulting.com/our-work/areas-of-expertise/inclusive-sponsorship/
9. Catalyst. Coaches, Mentors, and Sponsors: Understanding the Differences. New York: Catalyst, December 11, 2014.

2. Other Supportive Relationships

1. https://www.mckinsey.com/featured-insights/sustainable-inclusive-growth/future-of-america/freelance-side-hustles-and-gigs-many-more-americans-have-become-independent-workers
2. https://expandusbusinesscoaching.com/blog/coaching-mentoring-or-consulting-whats-the-right-fit-for-your-business/]

3. Structure and Categories of Mentorship

1. https://www.websitemagazine.com/blog/5-surprising-mentors-of-legendary-ceos
2. https://hrzone.com/its-time-to-get-rid-of-reverse-mentoring/
3. L. McKewon, "A Peer into Peer-to-Peer Mentoring, Expert Magazine 2002, http://bit.ly/1h36jNe)
4. **E.A. Ensher, C. Thomas, S.E. Murphy, "Comparison of traditional, step-ahead, and peer mentoring on proteges' support, satisfaction, and perceptions of career success: A social exchange perspective," *Journal of Business and Psychology*, 15 (3) 419-438 (2001).**
5. (Hershatter, A., Epstein, M. Millennials and the World of Work: An Organization and Management Perspective.*J Bus Psychol*25, 211–223 (2010). https://doi.org/10.1007/s10869-010-9160-y,
6. [1] Megginson D, Clutterbuck D (1995) Mentoring in Action: a practical guide for managers. Kogan Page, London
7. The Circle Way, found at https://www.thecircleway.net/
8. https://issuu.com/innovations2solutions/docs/2013_workplace_trends_report
9. https://files.eric.ed.gov/fulltext/ED467570.pdf
10. https://www.thebalancesmb.com/the-value-of-a-business-mentor-1200818

5. Roles and Responsibilities of a Mentor

1. https://www.lifeworkswell.ca/blog/eg45anmlcyaeg7xdet3j5r8xlhhyx9

6. Roles and Responsibilities of a Mentee

1. https://kdpworks.org/apprenticeships
2. Hodell, Chuck, ISD From the Ground Up Training, 2011, Association of Training and Development.
3. https://www.expandapprenticeship.org/system/files/mentoring_for_apprenticeship.pdf
4. See the Ontario Employment Standards Act, s. 3(5) https://www.ontario.ca/laws/statute/00e41#BK5.
5. https://www.marshallgoldsmith.com/articles/try-feedforward-instead-feedback/

7. Implementing a Mentor Program

1. https://www.purdueglobal.edu/education-partnerships/generational-workforce-differences-infographic/
2. https://www.purdueglobal.edu/education-partnerships/generational-workforce-differences-infographic/
3. https://www.togetherplatform.com/resources/business-case-for-mentoring and https://www.mentorcity.com/

8. The Business Case

1. Chase Consulting Group at https://www.chasegroup.com.au/; use lifeworkswell for a discount!
2. Chase Consulting Group at https://chasegroup.com.au/five-steps-to-develop-a-solid-business-case
3. Mentor Program Business Case at https://www.lifeworkswell.ca/mentorship-sponsorship-coaching
4. According to official Vistage publications, this survey polled 1,348 CEOs and found that 86% agreed mentors were a critical part of their career accomplishments. Currently 98% of the Fortune 500 companies have a mentor program according to the latest Mentor-Cliq Impact Report (in 2023 it was 92%) https://www.mentorcliq.com/ blog/mentoring-impact-report
5. (Catalyst, 1996; Dreher & Ash, 1990; Fagenson, 1989; Johnson & Scandura, 1994; Lankau & Scandura, 2002; Jones 2012; Chun et al, 2012
6. Allen, T. D., Eby, L. T., Poteet, M. L., Lentz, E., & Lima, L. (2004). Career benefits associated with mentoring for protégés: A meta-analysis. Journal of Applied Psychology, 89(1), 127–136. https://doi.org/10.1037/0021-9010.89.1.127
7. The state of mentoring research: A qualitative review of current research methods and future research implications.
   https://www.sciencedirect.com/science/article/abs/pii/S0001879107000747
8. Ibid (FN 6 and 7), as well as Hunt and Michael, 1983; Kram, 1985; Jones 2012; Chun et al, 2012
9. Dickinson, K., Jankot, T., & Gracon, H. (2009). Sun Mentoring: 1996–2009. Sun Microsystems Laboratories Technical Report SMLI TR-2009-185
10. Fagenson-Eland et al., 1997; Wilson and Elman, 1996
11. Hegstad, C. D., & Wentling, R. M. (2005). Organizational antecedents and moderators that impact on the effectiveness of exemplary formal mentoring programs in fortune 500 companies in the United States. *Human Resource Development International, 8*(4), 467–487. https://doi.org/10.1080/13678860500199808
12. (Knowledge at Wharton) https://knowledge.wharton.upenn.edu/podcast/knowl edge-at-wharton-podcast/workplace-loyalties-change-but-the-value-of-mentor ing-doesnt/; (ART OF MENTORING) https://artofmentoring.net/goal-setting-and-measuring-the-impact-of-mentoring/ and (Evidence-Based Mentoring) https://www.evidencebasedmentoring.org/what-great-mentorship-looks-like-in-a-hybrid-workplace/
13. Sun Mentoring: 1996–2009. Sun Microsystems Laboratories Technical Report SMLI TR-2009-185
14. Ibid.
15. Art of Mentoring as above.

9. How to Find a Mentor Outside Your Organization

1. https://www.centerformentoring.com/5457-2-2; and, Mitsuhashi, Y. (2018). *Ikigai.* Kyle Books.
2. YMCA Newcomer Information Centre

3. https://mosaicbc.org/our-programs/mentoring-programs-for-new-immigrants-in-canada/
4. https://canadianimmigrant.ca/featured/find-a-mentor
5. https://www.mentoringpartnership.ca/?gad_source=1&gclid=CjwKCAjwoaS3Bh A3EiwAKaD2ZSAsBeUG9WimWtTjqfo9KgKsLVPwMrrUlb-fAXfAvjAI7kC3BOVn2RoCbM8QAvD_BwE
6. https://canadianimmigrant.ca/featured/find-a-mentor
7. https://www.hrpa.ca/about-hrpa/the-hrpa-mentorship-program/
8. https://ama-toronto.com/mentor-exchange/
9. https://cmpa.ca/mentorship/

10. Create a Mentor World

1. Dr. Nava Israel, *Conetrolled, How we've lost our freedom and how to reclaim it (page 29)* https://www.navainc.ca/product-page/conetrolled-ebook
2. https://globalmentorship.org/
3. Jennifer Jones-Morales, Alison M. Konrad, (2018) "Attaining elite leadership: career development and childhood socioeconomic status", Career Development Internationa
4. https://jacanada.org/who-we-are
5. https://www.mentoringcanada.ca/en
6. https://www.mentoring.org/
7. https://blackmentorshipinc.ca/
8. https://www.mentorcity.com/
9. https://www.tenthousandcoffees.com/
10. https://www.tenthousandcoffees.com/schools
11. https://www.centerformentoring.com/
12. https://www.centerformentoring.com/bridging-differences and https://www.centerformentoring.com/thementorsguide
13. http://www.twomentor.com/white-paper-roi-mentoring
14. https://nationalmentoringday.org/
15. https://ugoimpact.com/
16. WIBN womeninbiznetwork.com; ChangeMaker Collective https://changemakerco.org/

ABOUT THE AUTHOR

Helen Patterson is the founder of Life Works Well, helping organizations build healthy, high-performance and heart-centered cultures where people thrive and businesses grow.

With over 20 years of experience across HR leadership, employment law, learning and development, and more, Helen blends her strategic people expertise with her passion for everyday mentorship. She has worked with leading Canadian brands including CIBC, ADP Canada, Canadian Media Producers, MI Concept and Design, Foot Locker, Champs, and The Northern Group, and now supports purpose-driven small and growing businesses across sectors. Helen was a professor of HR and former lead editor and author of two Thomson Reuters HR publications—Employment Policies that Work and Best Practice Terminations.

Mentorship is at the core of Helen's mission. A prior Chair of Mentorship for HRPA Toronto West and a Top 5 Mentor of the Year at Futurpreneur, she believes mentorship is built through the everyday moments that create belonging, confidence, and future leaders.

Outside her work, Helen can be found travelling, walking, enjoying sunrise and sunset views, spending time with her family and friends, or creating community through heart-centered conversations.

You can Connect with Helen here:

Website: **https://lifeworkswell.ca**

LinkedIn: **https://www.linkedin.com/in/lifeworkswell/**

Instagram: @lifeworkswell.ca